Life in the Fast-Food Lane

An ADAM Collection by Brian Basset
Foreword by Lynn Johnston

Andrews and McMeel A Universal Press Syndicate Company Kansas City • New York

ADAM is distributed internationally by Universal Press Syndicate.

ISBN: 0-8362-1873-6

Library of Congress Catalog Card Number: 90-85471

FOREWORD

The first time I read Adam, I had an overwhelming need to meet Brian Basset. When it comes to raising the next generation, it's not possible to write and draw with such insight unless one is in the front lines! I wanted to know how much of Adam was Brian himself.

As it happened, we met on a convention floor. Two strangers across a crowded room; our eyes met, our hands clasped—and except for his fiery red hair, the man behind the pen looked surprisingly familiar. Godzilla meets King Kong; Batman meets the Phantom; Elly Patterson meets Adam Newman! It was a joyous occasion of epic importance all-around.

Brian draws funny, and he writes well—two prime tools for survival in a world of household trivia and unpaid bills. The depth of feeling he pours into a look of total exasperation, the piercing stare of an embittered mate, the self-righteous sneer of an eight-year-old tells me he's been there—and *lived*! The ability to produce lines like "What do we owe the sitter?"—"Our eternal gratitude . . . and $25.00" is a rare and coveted gift . . . which he uses so well.

Brian Basset has my admiration as a cartoonist, as a parent, and as a friend.

Here, at long last is someone who really understands me!!

—Lynn Johnston

**FOR MY MOTHER AND FATHER,
WHO LET ME DRAW ON WALLS**

ADAM
BY BRIAN BASSET

ZAP

FASTEST DRAW IN THE WEST!
WOOOOSH!

RINNNNG
RINNNNNNG
RINNNNNNG

(CLICK) HI, I CAN'T COME TO THE PHONE RIGHT NOW— I'M BUSY MOPPING FLOORS, VACUUMING RUGS, CLEANING BATHROOMS, DUSTING FURNITURE, DOING LAUNDRY AND CHANGING DIAPERS.

SO IF YOU'LL LEAVE YOUR NAME AND MESSAGE AT THE BEEP, I'LL GET BACK TO YOU. THANKS.

BEEEEP.

THIS IS YOUR WIFE! QUIT WATCHING TV AND PICK UP THE PHONE!
BRIAN BASSET

I JUST WANT YOU TO KNOW THAT I MIGHT NOT BE HERE WHEN YOU GET HOME FROM WORK.
BRIAN BASSET

Y'SEE.. I NEED A BREAK FROM THE KIDS, SO I'M FLYING OFF TO THE SOUTH PACIFIC FOR A FEW MONTHS, AND THEN ON TO THE HIMALAYAS TO LIVE WITH TIBETAN MONKS FOR THE REMAINDER OF THE YEAR.
THAT'S NICE. I'LL SEE YA AROUND 5:30. LOVE YA, BYE.

DARN. HOW'D SHE KNOW I WAS BLUFF-ING?

CLAYTON! KATY! I JUST CLEANED THIS ROOM, AND IT'S A PIGSTY ALREADY!!

I SWEAR THE TWO OF YOU DESTROY A ROOM FASTER THAN I CAN PICK IT UP!!
BRIAN BASSET
THAT'S NOT SO!
YEAH, WE ALWAYS GIVE HIM AT LEAST A 10-MINUTE HEAD START.

LAURA, DO YOU EVER MISS THOSE DAYS WHEN WE WERE CHILD-FREE AND COULD DO JUST ABOUT ANYTHING?
LIKE GO TO DINNER WHEN-EVER WE WANTED?

OR SEE A MOVIE AND STAY OUT LATE!
BRIAN BASSET

AND TAKE A LONG TRIP ON A WHIM!!
NO, OF COURSE NOT.
ME NEITHER.

WHATCHA COOKING, DAD?
I'M TRYING OUT A NEW RECIPE FOR TUNA NOODLE SUPREME.

GEE, I THINK I'LL HAVE TO PASS. MY STOMACH'S STILL UPSET FROM LAST CHRISTMAS' FRUITCAKE.

BRIAN BASSET

I'M TRYING OUT A NEW EXCUSE FOR TUNA NOODLE SUPREME.

TREVOR'S MOM IS SERVING TACOS TONIGHT, DAD! I'M... I'M SURE THEY'D LET ME EAT OVER IF I WERE TO ASK!!
CLAYTON, IT WON'T KILL YOU TO EAT WHAT I MAKE!

I SUPPOSE YOU'RE RIGHT.

BRIAN BASSET
...OR I WOULD'VE BEEN A GONER YEARS AGO.

C'MON, ADAM, YOU'RE *NOT* A TERRIBLE CHEF!
BRIAN BASSET

MOST WOMEN WOULD DIE IF THEY HAD A HUSBAND LIKE YOU COOKING FOR THEM!

I MEAN, MOST WOMEN WOULD DIE **TO** HAVE A HUSBAND LIKE YOU COOKING FOR THEM!!

WHAT'S FOR DINNER, DADDY? TUNA NOODLE SUPREME?
OK, OK, I GET THE MESSAGE.
TUNA NOO

EVERYONE INTO THE CAR— WE'RE EATING OUT TONIGHT!
?
BRIAN BASSET

GOOD JOB, KATY! WHAT EXACTLY DID YOU SAY TO HIM??!
BEATS ME. I ONLY WISH NOW THAT I'D ASKED FOR A RAISE IN MY ALLOWANCE.
SLAP!

I THINK ADAM'S CONFIDENCE IN THE KITCHEN HAS REALLY BEEN SHAKEN.
BRIAN BASSET

THE KIDS WON'T EAT WHAT HE FIXES, EH?

MM-WORSE.

HE WON'T EVEN EAT WHAT HE FIXES.

FUNNY, I NEVER REALIZED JUST HOW THIN-SKINNED YOU WERE UNTIL THIS WEEK.

FIRST YOU GOT YOUR FEELINGS ALL HURT BECAUSE THE KIDS WOULDN'T TOUCH YOUR MEATLOAF.

AND THEN YOU BECAME INSULTED THAT MY MOM HAD THE "AUDACITY" TO SEND ME A CARE PACKAGE FULL OF FOOD.

GEE, AND I THOUGHT THE SENSITIVE MALE WAS "IN."
BRIAN BASSET

AHHHH. THIS IS THE TIME OF DAY I LOOK FORWARD TO.
WHEN THE KIDS ARE IN BED, THE HOUSE-WORK'S BEHIND ME, AND THE TWO OF US CAN *FINALLY* BE TOGETHER.

BRIAN BASSET
Z

NO, TELL US HOW YOU ***REALLY*** FEEL ABOUT STRAINED PEAS.
BRIAN BASSET

LAURA, QUICK! LOOK!
MILK

ADAM
BY BRIAN BASSET
HI, NICK NEWMAN HERE FOR HIS APPOINTMENT.
YOU'RE RIGHT ON TIME.

...THE DOCTOR WAS SUPPOSED TO SEE HIM 45 MINUTES AGO.

WAHHHHH HHHH HHHH
AHH-- CHOOO
HACK HACK COUGH

WAHHHHHH HHHHH
SNIFFLE SNIFFLE SNORT SNEEZE
COUGH COUGH HACK

MR. NEWMAN. WHEN DID YOU FIRST NOTICE NICK'S RUNNY NOSE AND CONSTANT COUGHING?

HUH?! HE'S ONLY HERE FOR A BOOSTER SHOT.

HHHH HHH HH
OH.
AHH... CHOOO!
I SUPPOSE THREE DAYS FROM NOW.
HACK HACK COUGH!
THANK YOU.
TYPE TYPE
BRIAN BASSET

WHAT'RE YOU WORKING ON?
TYPE TYPE TYPE

I'M STARTING UP A NEIGHBORHOOD NEWS-LETTER FOR US STAY-AT-HOME TYPES.

HERE. TAKE A LOOK AT THE FIRST ISSUE AND TELL ME WHAT YOU THINK.
BRIAN BASSET

THE "DUST RAG"?
CATCHY NAME, HUH? I THOUGHT IT UP MYSELF!

WHAT'S THIS?! YOU'VE WRITTEN AN EDITORIAL ABOUT THE HUCKLESTONES' SEPARATION?
SURE! IT WAS NEIGH-BORHOOD NEWS, AND THIS IS A NEIGHBOR-HOOD NEWSLETTER.

WONDERFUL! I SUPPOSE I CAN LOOK FORWARD TO READING ABOUT ANY PROBLEMS WE MIGHT ENCOUNTER ?!
BRIAN BASSET

YOU NEEDN'T WORRY, LAURA.
... MY COLUMN'S UNDER AN ASSUMED NAME.
TYPE TYPE TYPE

Talk around the neigh-borhood has it that Beth (not her real name) and her husband of...
TYPE TYPE TYPE TYPE

BRIAN BASSET
BEEP BOP BEEP BEEP BOOP

ELIZABETH! HI, IT'S ADAM. UM... JUST HOW LONG HAVE YOU AND JOHN BEEN MARRIED?
GOT IT. THANKS.

.. 16 years, Jack (not his real name), are having major marital....
TYPE TYPE TYPE TYPE

CAROL, HI, IT'S ADAM.

MIND IF I ASK YOU A FEW QUESTIONS FOR THE "DUST RAG"?.... GREAT!

MY READERS WOULD LIKE TO KNOW IF THERE'S ANY TRUTH TO THE RUMOR THAT YOUR SO-CALLED "FAMILY RECIPE" FOR DUTCH APPLE PIE WAS ACTUALLY TAKEN FROM A MAGAZINE?
UH-HUH.. UH-HUH.. GOT IT!
TYPE TYPE
BRIAN BASSET

WHAT'S THAT— YOU WANT ME TO READ IT BACK TO YOU?..
TYPE TYPE TYPE
"Don't you have anything better to do with your time?"

I'M IN KIND OF A HURRY! COULD I GET 12 COPIES OF THESE RIGHT AWAY?!
COPIES
NO PROBLEM.

"THE DUST RAG"?
YEAH. IT'S A NEIGHBORHOOD NEWSLETTER I JUST STARTED...
WHAT'S THIS?? SOME WOMAN SUSPECTS HER HUSBAND OF HAVING AN AFFAIR WITH MY WIFE?!
UH... NO RUSH ON THOSE.
BRIAN BASSET

BRIAN BASSET
LADIES, I OWE YOU AN APOLOGY.
YOU ENTRUSTED ME TO PUT TOGETHER THE FIRST ISSUE OF OUR NEWSLETTER.. AND ALL I DID WAS PRODUCE A SLEAZY, CHEAP TABLOID.

WHEN DOES THE SECOND ISSUE COME OUT?!

... AND A CHOCOLATE SHAKE.
GOT IT. GEE, SOUNDS LIKE YOU'VE GOT YOUR HANDS FULL.
BRIAN BASSET

YOU'RE TELLING ME! HAVE ANY KIDS OF YOUR OWN?
NO, BUT MY WIFE AND I WOULD LIKE TO START A FAMILY SOON.
DOES SHE WORK?
YEAH, SHE'S A NURSE. BUT I THINK SHE'D LIKE TO TAKE SOME TIME OFF WHEN WE HAVE A BABY.
THIS IS CRAZY. I'M HAVING A CONVERSATION WITH A BACON CHEESEBURGER.

HAVE I TOLD YOU LATELY WHAT A GREAT JOB YOU DO AROUND HERE?

...AND JUST HOW LUCKY I AM TO BE MARRIED TO YOU?

...AND HOW FORTUNATE THE KIDS ARE TO HAVE YOU FOR A FATHER?
BRIAN BASSET

YOUR RAISE DIDN'T COME THROUGH, HUH?

YOU GET BATH DUTY NEXT TIME.
BRIAN BASSET

ADAM
BY BRIAN BASSET

NOW THIS IS LIVING!
CLICK

?
CLICK
CLICK

CLICK
CLICK
CLICK
CLICK

CONFOUND IT! THE DUMB BATTERIES MUST BE DEAD IN THE REMOTE CONTROL!
WHACK
WHACK!
WHACK!!

AWWWW, I SUPPOSE THIS MEANS YOU'LL HAVE TO GET UP EVERY TIME YOU WANT TO CHANGE THE CHANNEL?.. POOR BABY.
HA-HA. VERY FUNNY.

BRIAN BASSET

BRIAN BASSET

WE'RE HERE!
GEE, I DIDN'T THINK YOU'D SHOW.

ARE YOU KIDDING? I'VE BEEN LOOKING FORWARD TO THIS ALL WEEK.
FACE IT, TOM. THERE'S NO WAY YOU'RE GOING TO OUT-DIAPER ME. SO NOW'S THE TIME TO BACK OUT.

IS THAT A LITTLE FEAR I DETECT IN YOUR VOICE?

HARDLY. I'M JUST TRYING TO KEEP YOUR SON FROM BEING LABELED A LOSER AT SUCH A TENDER AGE.

THAT DID IT! BREAK OUT THE DESITIN!!
BRIAN BASSET

SIMPLE RULES, NOTHING COMPLICATED. THE ONE WHO CHANGES THE DIAPER THE FASTEST WINS.

MY OLDER BOY, CLAYTON, WILL KEEP THE OFFICIAL TIME.

SAAAY, HOW DO I KNOW YOUR SON WON'T PLAY HOMETOWN FAVORITES?

BRIAN BASSET
DON'T WORRY. HE MADE ME EAT LIVER THE OTHER NIGHT.

SO TELL ME, ADAM— WHO WON THE BIG DIAPERING CONTEST?... YOU OR TOM??!
BRIAN BASSET

UH-OH. SOMETHING TELLS ME THAT IT WASN'T YOUR DADDY, NICK.
HE USED A DISPOSABLE, I USED CLOTH. IT WASN'T EVEN CLOSE.

TSK-TSK, ADAM. THIS ISN'T GOING TO LOOK GOOD ON OUR SON'S RÉSUMÉ.
GOOD LORD! I DIDN'T EVEN THINK OF THAT.

DOCTOR'S OFFICE, MAY I HELP YOU?

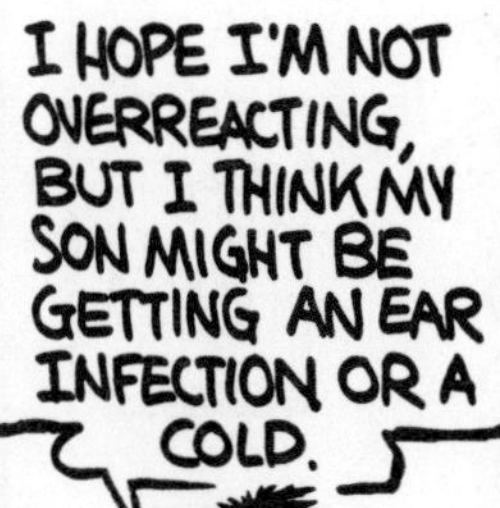
I HOPE I'M NOT OVERREACTING, BUT I THINK MY SON MIGHT BE GETTING AN EAR INFECTION OR A COLD.

TELL ME IF YOU THINK I AM! I MEAN — THE LAST THING I WANT TO SOUND LIKE IS ONE OF THOSE ALARMIST PARENTS.

THERE'S NO SUCH THING. IT'S ALWAYS BEST TO CALL.
BRIAN BASSET

IT'S MR. NEWMAN.
AGAIN?!

A HUNDRED DOLLARS IF YOU GIVE NICK HIS BATH TONIGHT.

OK, TWO HUNDRED DOLLARS IF YOU GIVE NICK HIS BATH!

THREE HUNDRED DOLLARS! THAT'S IT, THAT'S MY FINAL OFFER.... THREE HUNDRED DOLLARS!!

BRIAN BASSET
TOUGH DAY, HUH?

EVER SINCE I TOOK HIM TO THE PARK LAST WEEK, IT'S THE ONLY WAY HE'LL EAT HIS SPAGHETTI.
BRIAN BASSET

IF ANYONE HAS ANYTHING THAT NEEDS CLEANING — THROW IT DOWN NOW!

BRIAN BASSET

I MEANT LAUNDRY.

CLAYTON'S DAD IS A SISSY!!
YEAH, HE STAYS HOME CHANGING DIAPERS!

HA HA HA HA HA HA HA
BRIAN BASSET

?
GET A JOB!

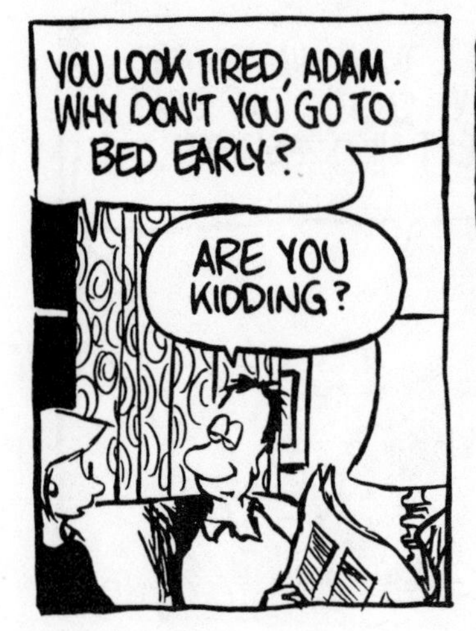
YOU LOOK TIRED, ADAM. WHY DON'T YOU GO TO BED EARLY?
ARE YOU KIDDING?

...THIS IS THE FIRST CHANCE I'VE HAD ALL DAY TO PUT MY FEET UP AND READ THE PAPER.

HOWEVER, A BACK-RUB SURE WOULD BE NICE ABOUT NOW.

BRIAN BASSET
IT SURE WOULD.

ADAM
BY BRIAN BASSET
LET'S EAT! I'M HUNGRY!
ME, TOO!
FINALLY... SOMETHING THEY CAN AGREE ON.

BURGERS!
TACOS!!

LET ME HAVE TWO SHIVER-ME-TIMBERS BURGERS, A 12-PIECE TREASURE CHEST OF NUGGETS, FOUR BAGS OF OL' SALTY FRIES, AND THREE YO-HO-HO AND A BOTTLE OF POPS.

DAD, I'VE CHANGED MY MIND. I THINK I'D RA
UH, HOLD ON.

NO, MAKE THAT ONLY ONE SHIVER-ME-TIMBER BURGER... ADD A JOLLY ROGER FISH FILET ON A BUN... STAY WITH THE NUGGETS.... MAKE ONE OF THOSE FRIES A LARGE, AND KEEP THE POPS THE SAME.
DAAAAD!

OK, OK, OK. CHANGE THE FISH FILET TO A YELLOW-BELLIED MUTINEER'S CHICKEN SANDWICH AND MAKE THE 12-PIECE NUGGETS A 9-PIECE.

OH, AND ONE CHOCOLATE MILK-SHAKE.

UH... NEVER MIND ON THE MILKSHAKE.

OH, AND DON'T FORGET—NICK HAS A DOCTOR'S APPOINTMENT TODAY!
WHAT TIME?

IT'S ON THE CALENDAR.
WHERE'S THE CALENDAR?
ON THE SIDE OF THE REFRIGERATOR WHERE IT'S ALWAYS BEEN!
THAT'S TODAY, RIGHT?

YES! NOW BEFORE I'M REALLY LATE FOR WORK, DO YOU HAVE ANY MORE QUESTIONS?!!
BRIAN BASSET

YES. ARE YOU GETTING ENOUGH SLEEP? YOU SEEM SO CRANKY.

C'MON, NICK! HOLD STILL.
BRIAN BASSET

WE'VE GOT TO (OOF) GET YOU DRESSED...

...SO WE CAN GO SEE THE (UMPH) DOCTOR!

YOU CAN TAKE YOUR SON TO EXAM ROOM 6, MR. NEWMAN... AND HAVE HIM GET UNDRESSED, PLEASE.

THIRD DOOR ON THE LEFT. THE DOCTOR WILL SEE YOUR SON NOW.

BRIAN BASSET

"NOW" MUST BE SHORT FOR NEVER OR WHENEVER.

AND HOW'S OUR LITTLE PATIENT TODAY?
EXAM RM. 6
FINE WHEN WE ARRIVED.
BUT HOW WOULD YOU FEEL IF YOU WERE COOPED UP IN A LITTLE ROOM FOR AN HOUR?
AN HOUR, YOU SAY?!.. GOOD GOD, MAN! DO YOU KNOW WHAT THIS MEANS?
NO, WHAT?
BRIAN BASSET
I'M EARLY FOR A CHANGE!

HOW'D NICK'S DOCTOR'S APPOINTMENT GO, ADAM?
IT WAS AWFUL! THE DOCTOR DIDN'T SHOW UP FOR OVER AN HOUR, AND WE HAD TO WAIT IN THIS TINY LITTLE ROOM WITHOUT ANY GOOD TOYS, MAGAZINES, OR...
BRIAN BASSET
NO! HOW'D NICK'S CHECKUP COME OUT?!
UH, FINE. THE DOC SAID HE'S IN GREAT SHAPE.
THANK YOU.
OH, AND GET THIS— WHEN HE FINALLY DID COME IN HE SAID THAT HE WAS ACTUALLY EARLY FOR ONCE, AND...

IS THAT MY LUNCH YOU'RE FIXING, DAD?
YUP! YOU'RE HAVING A PEANUT BUTTER AND JELLY SANDWICH.
UH... THINK YA COULD CARVE A BATMAN EMBLEM INTO THE BREAD?
I CAN SURE GIVE IT A TRY.
ISN'T THAT CUTE— HE WANTS A BATMAN EMBLEM.
BRIAN BASSET

BOY! THIS SHOULD REALLY INCREASE ITS VALUE FOR TRADING!

UM...I WAS THINKING OF GOING OUT WITH THE GUYS TONIGHT... WOULD THAT BE OK?
ABSOLUTELY.

IT'S JUST THAT I NEED A BREAK FROM THE KIDS EVERY NOW AND THEN.
I UNDERSTAND PERFECTLY.

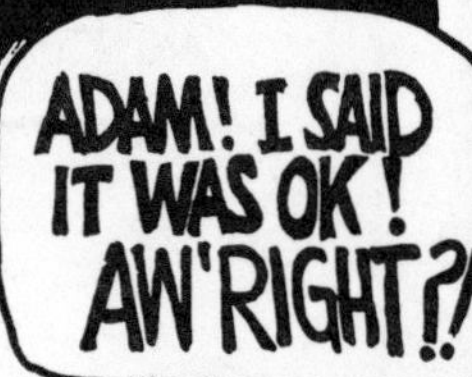
IT'S NOT LIKE I GET OUT A LOT, Y'KNOW...
ADAM! I SAID IT WAS OK! AW'RIGHT?!

BRIAN BASSET

WELL, HOW'D LAURA REACT?
SHE SEEMED PRETTY ANNOYED.

SO, WHAT'S THE PLAN OF ATTACK, GENTS?
WELL... I'VE NEVER BEEN THERE, BUT I'VE HEARD ABOUT THIS PLACE THAT HAS LAS VEGAS-STYLE SHOW-GIRLS WHO...
NO WAY! LAURA WOULD KILL ME!
(SIGH) SAME WITH MY WIFE.

BRIAN BASSET

LET'S DO IT!

COME ON! WHAT'RE WE WAITING FOR?—UNLESS, OF COURSE, EVERYONE'S AFRAID OF WHAT THEIR WIVES MIGHT SAY?!
SHOWGIRLS
BRIAN BASSET

DON'T BE SILLY! IT'S JUST THAT, WELL...... IT SAYS "NO ONE UNDER 18 ADMITTED," AND WOULDN'T YOU KNOW IT— I LEFT MY I.D. AT HOME!

GEE. SAME HERE.
DARN! ME, TOO.

I'M SORRY, YOU GUYS... I, I JUST CAN'T GO IN THERE.
GEESH, ADAM. DON'T RUIN IT FOR ALL OF US.
YEAH! DON'T BE SUCH A KILLJOY.
SHOWGIRLS
BRIAN BASSET

WELL, WHAT DO YOU PROPOSE?

C'MON! THIS WAY!
?

HEY, WHERE'S HE GOING?
IT'S JUST A LITTLE HARMLESS FUN, ADAM!
SORRY, GANG. I JUST CAN'T.
SHOWGIRLS

I FEEL LIKE A DIRTY OLD MAN. AND BESIDES— IT'S EXPLOITIVE OF WOMEN.

COME ON. LET'S GET OUT OF HERE BEFORE SOMEONE RECOGNIZES US.
YEAH!
ADAM! WAIT UP!
BRIAN BASSET

YOU'RE BACK EARLY. WHAT HAPPENED TO YOUR "BOYS NIGHT OUT"?

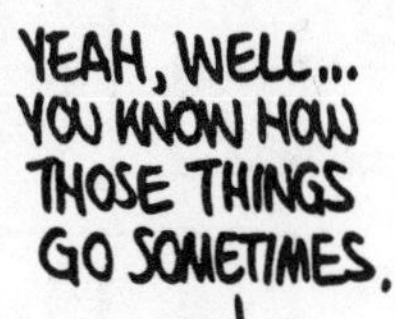
YEAH, WELL... YOU KNOW HOW THOSE THINGS GO SOMETIMES.

BRIAN BASSET
YOU WENT TO A TOPLESS JOINT AND YOU'RE RACKED WITH GUILT, RIGHT?
WE ONLY GOT AS FAR AS THE PARKING LOT! HONEST!!

ADAM
BY BRIAN BASSET
!

BRIAN BASSET

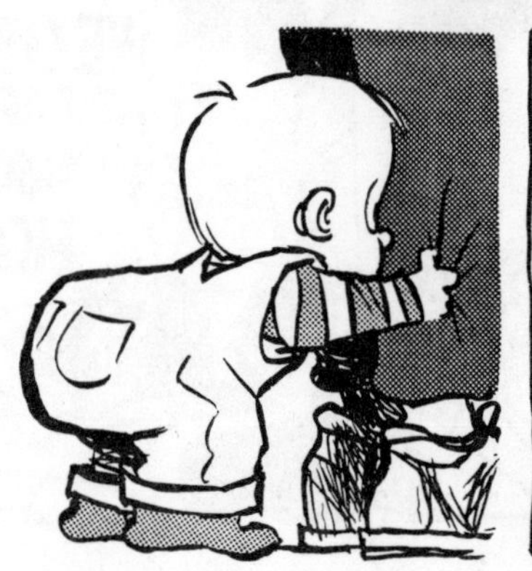

LOST THE DRAW-STRING TO YOUR SWEATS, I SEE.

REALLY? AND WHAT DID LAURA THINK OF IT?
SHE THOUGHT IT WAS A BIT SLOW IN PLACES, BUT...
...AND ADD A CUP OF SUGAR AND MAYBE A FEW CHOCOLATE CHIPS...
THAT SOUNDS GOOD. I'LL HAVE TO TRY IT.
BRIAN BASSET

TERRIFIC! ADAM'S LITTLE BOY HAS AN AWFUL RUNNY NOSE!
I CAN'T BELIEVE SHE EVEN CAME! HER SWEET LITTLE ASHLEY HAS A TERRIBLE COLD!!
THAT JASON JUST COUGHED ALL OVER MY EMILY!
GREAT! HER LITTLE GIRL IS ALWAYS SICK!

DID YOU REMEMBER TO PICK UP SOME SHAMPOO WHEN YOU WENT SHOP-PING TODAY, ADAM?

BRIAN BASSET
SMACK!
YOU DIDN'T, DID YOU?
WORSE. I FORGOT TO DO THE SHOPPING.

BRIAN BASSET
MICROWAVING POPCORN. WHY?

UGHH, TRAFFIC WAS A MESS! I DON'T THINK I HAVE TIME TO CHANGE... AND **YOU**— **YOU'D** BETTER GET **READY**!!
?

...THE SITTER SHOULD BE HERE **ANY** MINUTE.

COME ON, HURRY! YOU ACT AS IF YOU'VE FORGOTTEN WE HAVE A PARTY TO GO TO.
BRIAN BASSET

NOW **WHERE** IS THAT SITTER?!.... **WHAT TIME DID YOU TELL HER TO BE HERE, ADAM?**

YOU MUST BE LAURA'S HUSBAND, ADAM... THE HOUSEHUSBAND!
HOUSEHUSBAND?... NO, NOT EXACTLY.

NO? BUT DOWN AT THE OFFICE LAURA'S TOLD EVERYONE THAT YOU...
I KNOW, I KNOW... BUT Y'SEE WE'RE BOTH IN THE WITNESS RELOCATION PROGRAM, AND IT'S THE COVER THEY CAME UP FOR ME.
BRIAN BASSET
WOW! I HAD NO IDEA.

THERE YOU ARE! SO, ARE YOU HAVING A GOOD TIME AT THE PARTY?
VERY MUCH!

TERRIFIC PARTY. BUT HOW COME NO ONE FROM OUR GENERATION EVER DOES ANYTHING REALLY STUPID AT PARTIES— LIKE WHEN OUR PARENTS WERE YOUNG?
BRIAN BASSET

..Y'KNOW, SUCH AS STICKING A LAMPSHADE ON THEIR HEAD OR SOMETHING.

OH, I DON'T KNOW. WHAT D'YA CALL YOU AND BILL LYING ON YOUR BACKS SHOOTING CORKS OUT YOUR MOUTHS?

THAT WAS NOT STUPID! I KNEW I COULD HIT THE CEILING AND WIN THE FIVE DOLLARS.

YOUR HUSBAND PHONED AGAIN WHILE YOU WERE AT LUNCH, MRS. NEWMAN, AND LEFT A MESSAGE.

BRIAN BASSET
BEEP
BOP
BEEP
BEEP
I HAD THE SALMON IN A CUCUMBER BUTTER SAUCE, WITH NEW POTATOES AND BABY ASPARAGUS...
SIGH

ADAM, RIGHT?!
UH, RIGHT.

YOU MAY NOT REMEMBER ME, BUT MY HUSBAND AND I WERE IN THE SAME CHILDBIRTH CLASS WITH YOU AND YOUR WIFE.

YES OF COURSE! AND I SEE YOU'RE EXPECTING AGAIN.
BRIAN BASSET

NOOOO...
GEE, THAT'S A NICE STROLLER YOU HAVE THERE!

WAHHHHHHHHHHHHH
MENU

ADAM
BY BRIAN BASSET

PSSSST, CLAYTON. WHAT DID YOU GET FOR NUMBER SIX?

UH... 28.
YEAH!... ME, TOO!

PSSST, DONALD. WHAT DID YOU GET FOR NUMBER SEVEN?
36.

THANKS.

PSSSST, TOMMY. WHAT ANSWER DID YOU GET FOR NUMBER SEVEN?
36.

THANKS.

PSSSST, PATRICK. WHAT DID YOU COME UP WITH FOR NUMBER SEVEN?
36.

THANKS.

PSSSST, CLAYTON. WHAT DID YOU GET FOR NUMBER SEVEN?
36.

THANKS.

ADAM
BY BRIAN BASSET
THE KIDS ARE SO GREAT! THEY DIDN'T FORGET THAT TODAY IS FATHER'S DAY!

HOW COULD THEY? YOU'VE ONLY BEEN REMINDING THEM FOR THE PAST THREE WEEKS.

HERE. THIS IS FOR YOU.
WHAT?? NO, REALLY?!

GO AHEAD, OPEN IT.
LAURA! YOU DIDN'T HAVE TO, Y'KNOW. THE KIDS FIXED ME A GREAT BREAKFAST THIS MORNING!

HAPPY FATHER'S DAY!
A GIFT CERTIFICATE FOR A MASSAGE, SAUNA... AND A BODY SHAMPOO??!

YOU NEVER TREAT YOURSELF TO ANYTHING, ADAM... AND I KNOW WHAT IT'S LIKE HAULING A BABY AROUND ALL DAY.

NOW GO BEFORE YOU'RE LATE FOR YOUR APPOINTMENT WITH LESLIE!
LESLIE?!

S-S-S-S-S-S-S-S-S-SO Y-Y-Y-Y-Y-Y-Y-Y-YOU'RE L-L-L-L-L-L-L-L-LESLIE?
FRIENDS CALL ME LES.
BRIAN BASSET

BOP
BEEP
BEEP
BEEP

I MAY FORGET MY ANNIVERSARY OR MY SOCIAL SECURITY NUMBER, OR EVEN THE STREET I LIVE ON...

BETH! HI, IT'S ADAM. I REALIZE THIS IS RATHER SHORT NOTICE, BUT COULD I DROP NICK OFF AT YOUR PLACE FOR A FEW HOURS?!
...BUT I **NEVER** FORGET WHO OWES ME BABY-SITTING.

LUNCH TODAY, LAURA?
I CAN'T, CAROL. ADAM'S MEETING ME DOWNTOWN FOR LUNCH.

I THOUGHT I'D TAKE HIM TO THAT NEW HEALTH FOOD RESTAURANT ON PINE STREET.
SOUNDS GOOD!
YEAH! SINCE HE DOESN'T GET OUT OF THE HOUSE MUCH, I THOUGHT IT WOULD BE A NICE CHANGE FROM BEING AROUND BABY FOOD ALL DAY.

THIS STUFF'S LIKE **BABY FOOD!**

THIS IS NICE. I'M GLAD YOU COULD COME DOWNTOWN AND MEET ME FOR LUNCH, ADAM. BY THE WAY— WHO'S WATCHING NICK?
UH... NO ONE.
NO ONE? NO ONE?

IT'S NO BIG DEAL. I'VE LEFT HIM ALONE FOR LONGER PERIODS THAN THIS.

HA-HA. HAD YOU GOING THERE!

NO MORE PENCILS, NO MORE BOOKS, NO MORE TEACHER'S DIRTY LOOKS!!
SCHOOL BUS

BRIAN BASSET
SCHOOL BUS

SCHOOL BUS

NO MORE PENCILS, NO MORE BOOKS, NO MORE BUS DRIVER'S DIRTY LOOKS!!

LET'S GO OVER A FEW GROUND RULES FIRST.

THERE'S TO BE ABSOLUTELY NO RUNNING, YELLING, BICKERING, OR ROUGH-HOUSING WHILE YOUR BABY BROTHER IS NAPPING.
BRIAN BASSET

SO I SUGGEST YOU FAMILIARIZE YOURSELF WITH HIS NAP SCHEDULE AND COMMIT IT TO MEMORY.

WHEN DOES SCHOOL START UP AGAIN?!!
NOT FOR 82 DAYS. I DON'T KNOW IF I CAN MAKE IT THAT LONG.
SEPT.

CLAP
CLAP
CLAP

WELL, WELL, WELL. IF IT ISN'T THE MAN OF LEISURE.
WHEN ARE YOU GOING TO GET A REAL JOB AND QUIT MASQUERADING AS A SO-CALLED HOUSEHUSBAND?
GEEESH! ANYONE CAN PUNCH A FEW BUTTONS ON A WASHER AND DRYER.
WHAT'S FOR DINNER?! I'M STARVED!
WELL, WELL, WELL. IF IT ISN'T THE MAN OF LEISURE.
FLOP!
BRIAN BASSET

WALTER, I OVERHEARD WHAT YOU SAID TO ADAM AS YOU WERE COMING UP THE WALK, AND I THINK YOU OWE HIM AN APOLOGY.
APOLOGIZE? APOLOGIZE FOR WHAT?
ALL I DID WAS MAKE SOME HARMLESS LITTLE REMARK ON WHAT AN EASY JOB HE HAS PLAYING HOUSE ALL DAY WHILE WORKING STIFFS LIKE ME TRY TO EKE OUT A LIVING.
IF YOU WANT MY OPINION, THAT FREELOADER'S THE ONE WHO OWES ME AN APOLOGY!
I TAKE THAT BACK— YOU WON'T HAVE TIME TO APOLOGIZE... CONSIDERING YOU'LL BE DOING YOUR OWN WASH THIS WEEK.
BRIAN BASSET

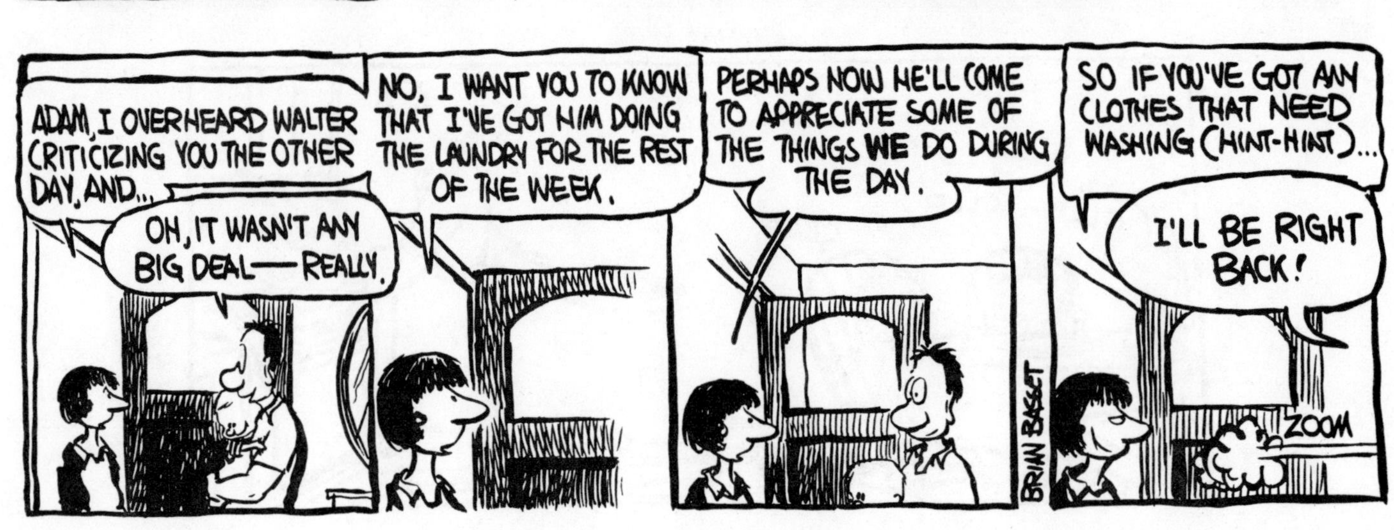
ADAM, I OVERHEARD WALTER CRITICIZING YOU THE OTHER DAY, AND...
OH, IT WASN'T ANY BIG DEAL— REALLY.
NO, I WANT YOU TO KNOW THAT I'VE GOT HIM DOING THE LAUNDRY FOR THE REST OF THE WEEK.
PERHAPS NOW HE'LL COME TO APPRECIATE SOME OF THE THINGS WE DO DURING THE DAY.
SO IF YOU'VE GOT ANY CLOTHES THAT NEED WASHING (HINT-HINT)...
I'LL BE RIGHT BACK!
ZOOM
BRIAN BASSET

OK, BETTY, WHAT GIVES? THIS IS NOT MY UNDERWEAR!

AND THAT'S NOT YOUR SOCK EITHER—IT'S ADAM'S. I JUST THOUGHT YOU MIGHT APPRECIATE YOUR NEIGHBOR A TAD MORE IF YOU HAD TO DO HIS LAUNDRY, TOO.
NEVER JUDGE A MAN UNTIL YOU'VE WALKED A MILE IN HIS SHOES.
BRIAN BASSET

OK, BUT NO WAY AM I DOING IT IN HIS SOCKS OR UNDERWEAR!

ADAM, I JUST WANTED TO COME OVER AND TELL YOU WHAT AN ADMIRABLE JOB YOU'RE DOING STAYING HOME WITH YOUR KIDS WHILE LAURA WORKS.

...AND ALSO TO APOLOGIZE FOR GIVING YOU SUCH A HARD TIME ABOUT IT THE OTHER DAY.

APOLOGY ACCEPTED.
BRIAN BASSET

OH, AND COULD I BORROW YOUR LAWN MOWER?!

ADAM
BY BRIAN BASSET
HMMM, TOUGH CHOICE.

I CAN WATCH EITHER A MOVIE I HAVEN'T SEEN SINCE I WAS A KID.... OR ONE THAT MY PARENTS WOULDN'T LET ME WATCH WHEN I WAS A KID.

HE'S HIGHLIGHTING TELEVISION SHOWS... I'M MARRIED TO A MAN WHO HIGHLIGHTS TELEVISION SHOWS!
BRIAN BASSET

SO WHAT'S IT LIKE HAVING YOUR HUSBAND HOME DURING THE DAY?
IT'S NICE.

ESPECIALLY FOR THE CHILDREN. THEY'RE THE ONES WHO *REALLY* BENEFIT.
BRIAN BASSET

PAY UP! I FINISHED CLEANING THE BATHROOM.
OK, OK. BUT REMEMBER, NO TELLING YOUR MOM.

GREAT MEAL, DAD!

PSSST, HAVE YOU NOTICED— *THAT'S* THE SIXTH TIME TONIGHT CLAYTON'S COMPLIMENTED MY COOKING.
BRIAN BASSET

AND YOU'VE ALWAYS SAID HIS APPRECIATION WASN'T GENUINE.

GREAT MEAL, DAD!

HA! YOU MISSED ME!!
BRIAN BASSET

TERRIFIC! TRAFFIC'S AT A SNAIL'S PACE AND I'M ALREADY 10 MINUTES LATE TO MY MEETING.

THIS DAY IS NOT GETTING OFF TO A VERY GOOD START.

OH, WELL. THEY SAY IF YOU EAT A TOAD FIRST THING IN THE MORNING, NOTHING WORSE CAN HAPPEN TO YOU THE REST OF THE ...

BRIAN BASSET
..DAY!
SMASH!

OK, LAURA. JUST TELL THEM THE TRUTH.
EXECUTI
CONFERE
ROOM

JUST TELL THEM HOW YOUR 1-YEAR-OLD FLUNG BABY CEREAL ACROSS THE ROOM THIS MORNING...
BRIAN BASSET

... NAILING YOUR NEW SUIT AND FORCING YOU TO COMPLETELY REWORK YOUR OUTFIT.

SORRY I'M LATE, EVERYONE. I GOT STUCK BEHIND THIS 26-CAR PILEUP ON THE FREEWAY.
EXECUTIVE
CONFERENCE
ROOM

I FEEL AWFUL! HOW COULD I HAVE LIED TO EVERYONE?

WHY COULDN'T I HAVE JUST TOLD THE TRUTH? INSTEAD I WENT AND MADE UP SOME RIDICULOUS STORY AS TO WHY I WAS LATE FOR THE MEETING.

BRIAN BASSET
(SIGH)
I FEEL AWFUL.

...AND LAURA, HOW DO YOU FEEL ABOUT THE PETERSON ACQUISITION?
AWFUL.

YOU WANTED TO SEE ME, R.W.?
PLEASE—— SIT DOWN, LAURA.
THIS MORNING YOU SPOKE OUT AGAINST THE PETERSON MERGER- A PROJECT, I MIGHT ADD, THAT I'VE BEEN PERSONALLY INVOLVED IN FOR OVER A YEAR.
IF YOU'LL LET ME EXPLAIN...
THAT WON'T BE NECESSARY— FOR YOU'VE JUST SAVED THIS COMPANY MILLIONS.
Y'SEE, I WAS EVEN HAVING DOUBTS MYSELF, AND, WELL, YOU ONLY CONFIRMED THEM. HERE, YOU'VE EARNED YOURSELF A SUBSTANTIAL BONUS.
BRIAN BASSET
IS THIS A GREAT COUNTRY OR WHAT?!

HOW WAS YOUR DAY?
BIZARRE.
I ZONED OUT AND REAR-ENDED SOME-ONE ON THE FREEWAY THIS MORNING, WAS 25 MINUTES LATE FOR MY MEETING...
...ACCIDENTALLY PANNED THE CEO'S PET PROJECT, THOUGHT I WAS GOING TO GET FIRED, AND INSTEAD ENDED UP GETTING A BIG BONUS FOR SAVING THE COMPANY MILLIONS.
BRIAN BASSET
AND SHE SAYS I WATCH TOO MANY SOAPS?

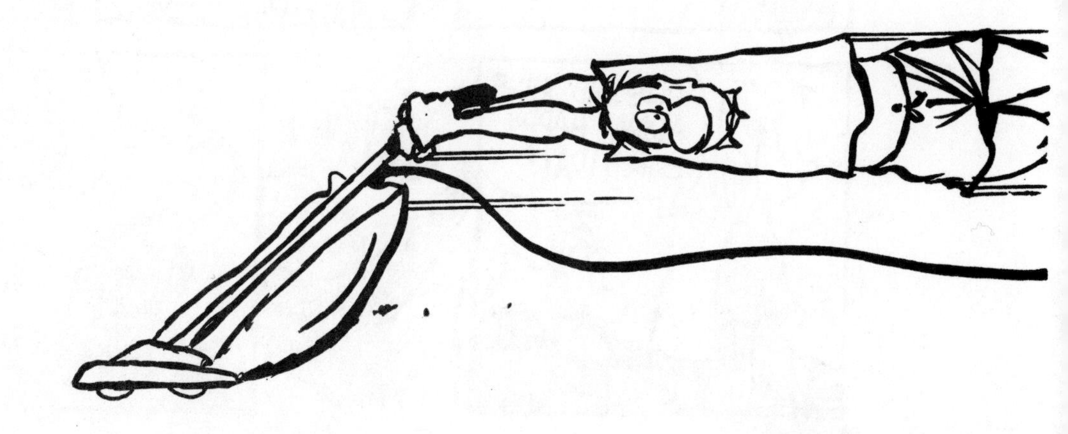

ADAM
BY BRIAN BASSET
WHIMPER WHIMPER

WOOF WOOF-WOOF WOOF...

ZZZZZ
6:50
TV

6:50

BRIAN BASSET

RISE AND SHINE, ADAM! HAPPY BIRTHDAY!

YAWN

HOW NICE TO SLEEP IN.... EVEN IF IT IS ONLY ONE DAY A YEAR.
9:51

ADAM
BY BRIAN BASSET
WHAT DO WE OWE THE SITTER?
OUR ETERNAL GRATITUDE.

AND $25.

WE'RE HOME. WELL... HOW WERE THE KIDS?
THEY WERE WONDERFUL, MRS. NEWMAN!

SHE MUST HAVE OUR CHILDREN CONFUSED WITH SOMEONE ELSE'S.

REALLY, THEY WERE GREAT! THEY GAVE ME NO PROBLEMS AT ALL.
G'BYE, MR. AND MRS. NEWMAN. THANKS FOR CALLING ME.

MAYBE WE'RE LIVING IN SOME WEIRD TWILIGHT-ZONE-LIKE EPISODE, AND THOSE REALLY AREN'T OUR CHILDREN UPSTAIRS.
BRIAN BASSET

ZOOM

NOPE. THEY'RE OURS.
Z

CLAYTON! WANT TO MAKE SOME MONEY?
YEAH— SURE!!

GREAT! I'LL PAY YOU A DOLLAR FOR EVERY BAG OF WEEDS YOU PICK.
BRIAN BASSET

WEEDS?
RATS. I THOUGHT YOU WERE TALKING ABOUT COUNTERFEITTING.

NO, NO, NO! THE WHOLE IDEA IS TO PICK THE DANDELIONS THAT ARE GROWING— NOT SPREAD NEW ONES!

THAT'S WHY DAD'S PAYING US A DOLLAR A BAGFUL.

BRIAN BASSET
I KNOW!

OK, YOU CAN PAY ME MY DOLLAR!...I PICKED A BAG OF WEEDS!

CLAYTON, THAT BAG'S HALF EMPTY.

BRIAN BASSET

THEY'VE COMPOSTED?

Y'KNOW, IT DOESN'T GET MUCH BETTER THAN THIS!

BRIAN BASSET

IT DOESN'T?!

UH-OH, YOU HAVE THAT LOOK ON YOUR FACE——WHAT WENT WRONG TODAY?
BRIAN BASSET

OH, NICK MUST'VE HID THE CHANNEL CHANGER. I HAVEN'T BEEN ABLE TO WATCH ANYTHING BUT THIS ONE STATION!

HMMM...
SIT UP!

SIT UP?...
HEY! LOOK AT THAT!!

GEESH! CAN YOU BELIEVE ALL THE JUNK THEY PUT IN THESE THINGS THESE DAYS?!
MUNCH
MUNCH
MUNCH
BRIAN BASSET

I KNOW! JUST HOW GOOD CAN STUFF LIKE SODIUM CITRATE, MONO-DIGLYCERIDE AND MALIC ACID REALLY BE FOR YOU?!

MUNCH
CRUNCH
MUNCH
NO, I WAS TALKING ABOUT THESE DUMB PLASTIC TRINKETS.

ADAM
BY BRIAN BASSET
DAD, WHAT WAS IT LIKE WHEN YOU WERE A KID?
WELL, FOR ONE THING, WE DIDN'T HAVE VCRS.

WOW.
WOW.

GRANDMA SAYS YOU WERE A REALLY GOOD KID, DAD.
...BUT DIDN'T YOU EVER DO ANYTHING BAD?... Y'KNOW, LIKE MAKING PRANK PHONE CALLS?
PRANK CALLS? ME?? NEVER!

WELL... (HEH-HEH) MAYBE JUST A FEW TIMES.

THEY WERE PRETTY HARMLESS, REALLY. I'D DIAL SOME NUMBERS AT RANDOM AND ASK WHOEVER ANSWERED IF (HEH-HEH) THEIR (HO-HO) REFRIGERATOR WAS RUNNING.

...AND IF THEY SAID "YES," I'D TELL 'EM...
THEN YOU'D BETTER HURRY UP AND CATCH IT!!

HA HA HA HA HA HA HA HA
HA HA HA HA HA HA
HA HA

SEE. I TOLD YOU HE'LL UNDERSTAND.
BRIAN BASSET

ADAM
BY BRIAN BASSET
DON'T SPLASH ME AGAIN, CLAYTON!

DID SHE SAY "DON'T"?

SPLASH

IF YOU SPLASH ME ONE MORE TIME I'M GOING TO TELL DAD!
BRIAN BASSET

BIG DEAL! IT'LL JUST BE YOUR WORD AGAINST MINE.
OH YEAH?!

YEAH!
YEAH?
YEAH!
YEAH?
YEAH!

SPLOSH

OOPS.

LAURA, DON'T GET ME WRONG. IT'S NOT THAT I DON'T WANT TO USE YOUR FREQUENT-FLIER COUPONS ON A FAMILY VACATION...

IT'S JUST THAT, WELL— WHEN YOU'RE LOCKED IN THE HOUSE SEVEN DAYS A WEEK WITH THE SAME CIRCUMSTANCES IT GETS OLD!

...AND TIME AWAY FROM CHILDREN IS VERY APPEALING.
BRIAN BASSET

I SEE YOUR POINT, ADAM. OK.
YOU CAN STAY HOME WHILE I TAKE THE KIDS TO DISNEYWORLD.

ACTUALLY, THE IDEA OF MY STAYING HOME WHILE LAURA HAULS THE KIDS TO DISNEYWORLD DOESN'T SOUND SO BAD.

NO DIAPERS TO CHANGE. NO ONE TO PICK UP AFTER. NO MEALS TO FIX.
BRIAN BASSET

I COULD STAY UP AS LATE AS I WANTED AND SLEEP IN EVERY MORNING.

YOU'RE SURE ABOUT YOUR DECISION?
YES. AS MUCH AS I'D LIKE TO COME, I THINK THIS WOULD BE A GOOD CHANCE FOR YOU TO SPEND SOME QUALITY TIME WITH THE KIDS.

DID YOU HEAR ?! MOM SAYS WE'RE GOING TO DISNEYWORLD THIS SUMMER !!

WE GET TO RIDE IN AN AIRPLANE!

THAT'S GREAT! BUT I HAVE SOMETHING TO TELL YOU. DADDY PROBABLY WON'T BE GOING. THIS WILL BE MOMMY'S CHANCE TO SPEND SOME SPECIAL TIME WITH YOU.
BRIAN BASSET

MY... THEY'RE TAKING IT WELL.

AW'RIGHT! WE'RE GOING TO DISNEYWORLD!
AND WE GET TO RIDE IN AN AIRPLANE!

DAD. WANT ME TO BRING YOU BACK A MICKEY MOUSE T-SHIRT OR SOMETHING FROM DISNEY WORLD?
SURE!

OH, RIGHT.
BRIAN BASSET

MORE?! I JUST GAVE YOU A TWENTY!
HANDLING CHARGE.

ADAM! TELEPHONE!
FIND OUT WHO IT IS AND WHAT THEY WANT.

UH-HUH... UH-HUH.

IT'S NORM, AND HE WANTS TO KNOW IF THE BIG POKER GAME YOU'RE HOSTING IS THE NIGHT AFTER I TAKE THE KIDS TO DISNEY WORLD, OR THE NIGHT BEFORE WE COME HOME.
BRIAN BASSET

ZIP

WHAT'S... THIS?!
MY NEW SWIMSUIT I'M TAKING TO FLORIDA, SILLY.

YOU CAN'T WEAR SOMETHING LIKE THAT OUT IN PUBLIC, LAURA!
BRIAN BASSET

OH? AND WHY NOT?

YOU'RE-YOU'RE A MOM FOR CRYING OUT LOUD!

WELL, IT'S ALMOST HERE. LAURA AND THE KIDS LEAVE FOR DISNEY WORLD TOMORROW.

AND A WHOLE WEEK OF PEACE AND QUIET WILL BE MINE.
ADAM, GO TO SLEEP.

BRIAN BASSET

HURRY UP, LAURA! THE KIDS ARE OUT IN THE CAR WAITING.

WAHHHH
BRIAN BASSET

BOY, AM I GLAD I DON'T HAVE TO LISTEN TO THAT FOR A WEEK!

NICK'S NOT GOING. HE'S RUNNING A TEMP, AND I THINK HE HAS AN EAR INFECTION.
WAHHHH

HA-HA, VERY FUNNY. AND WHY IS HE STILL IN HIS JAMMIES? I THOUGHT YOU PICKED OUT THAT CUTE BLUE AND GREEN OUTFIT FOR NICK TO WEAR ON THE PLANE.
WAHHHH

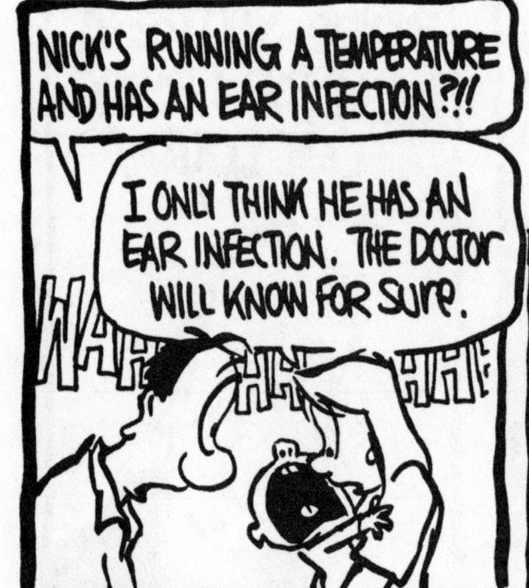
NICK'S RUNNING A TEMPERATURE AND HAS AN EAR INFECTION?!!
I ONLY THINK HE HAS AN EAR INFECTION. THE DOCTOR WILL KNOW FOR SURE.

BUT THERE ISN'T ENOUGH TIME TO MAKE YOUR FLIGHT AND HAVE NICK SEEN BY A DOCTOR!
RIGHT. ONE OF US WON'T BE GOING.
WAHHHH

WON'T BE GO---? OH, OHH, I GET IT.
BRIAN BASSET

YOU WANT ME TO TAKE YOUR PLACE AND GO TO FLORIDA WHILE YOU STAY HOME WITH NICK.
WAHHH

FINALLY! I THOUGHT HE'D NEVER STOP SCREAMING AND FALL ASLEEP.

TALK ABOUT ROTTEN TIMING. NICK GETS AN EAR INFECTION AND HAS TO STAY HOME WHILE LAURA'S OFF TO FLORIDA WITH THE OTHER TWO KIDS.

(SIGH) AND THERE GOES MY WEEK OF REST AND RELAXATION.
KLUNK

WHY ME? ME? ME? ME? ME? ME? ME?...
THUD
BRIAN BASSET

WAHHHHHHHH

WELL, WE'RE HERE, ADAM! READY FOR THE Poker GAME TO BEGIN.
Poker GAME? OH, RIGHT.

MAN, YOU LOOK AWFUL, ADAM. WHAT HAPPENED TO ALL THAT R&R YOU TALKED ABOUT GETTING WHILE LAURA AND THE KIDS WERE IN FLORIDA?

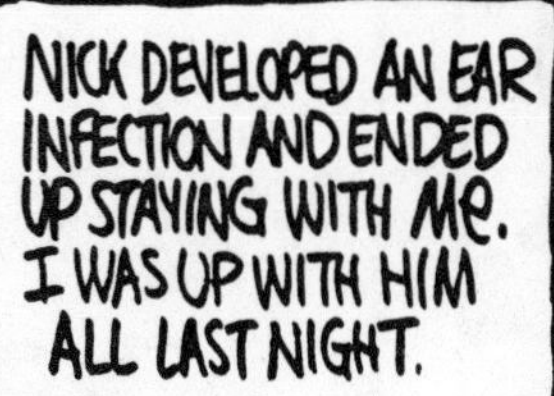
NICK DEVELOPED AN EAR INFECTION AND ENDED UP STAYING WITH ME. I WAS UP WITH HIM ALL LAST NIGHT.
BRIAN BASSET

GEE. MAYBE WE SHOULD GO.
NONSENSE. HE'S ONLY BLUFFING. TRYING TO PSYCH US OUT.
ZZZZ

I FOLD.
ME TOO. I'M OUT.
WHOA. IT'S ALMOST 6 A.M.! THAT'S IT FOR ME.
ZZZZ

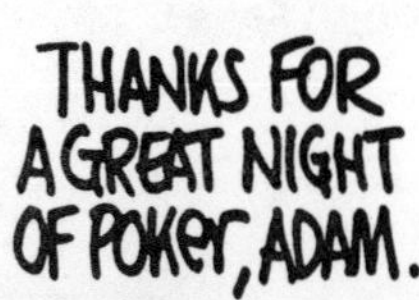
THANKS FOR A GREAT NIGHT OF Poker, ADAM.

YEAH. PERHAPS YOU'LL HAVE BETTER LUCK NEXT TIME. NOW GET SOME REST!
ZZ
HUH?

BRIAN BASSET
WAHHHHHHHHHHHH

THE KIDS HAVE HAD A WONDERFUL TIME AT DISNEY WORLD. I'M JUST SORRY NICK COULDN'T HAVE MADE IT.
ME TOO.

KATY HAD HER PICTURE TAKEN WITH MINNIE MOUSE TODAY! SO— HOW ARE THINGS ON YOUR END?
MY END?
BRIAN BASSET

I THINK WE MUST HAVE A BAD CONNECTION, ADAM...

...I CAN BARELY HEAR YOU.

WHERE'S DAD AND NICK?
I THOUGHT THEY WERE GOING TO MEET OUR PLANE AT THE GATE.
SO DID I.

I'LL PHONE HOME. I HOPE THEY DIDN'T FORGET.

NO ANSWER. I'LL BET THEY'RE WAITING FOR US OUT IN FRONT OF BAGGAGE CLAIM!

BRIAN BASSET
RINNGGG
RINNGGG
RINGGG

KNOCK KNOCK
DING DONG
COMING COMING
DING DONG
KNOCK! KNOCK!!

SORRY, BUT I DON'T (YAWN) HAVE ANY CANDY.

BRIAN BASSET
SLAM

KNOCK KNOCK
DING DONG
DING DONG
GEEEESH! THEY'RE GONNA WAKE THE BABY!

C'MON, DAD! GET A HIT!!
ADAM
BY BRIAN BASSET

...DON'T EMBARRASS THE FAMILY.

GET A HIT, DAD! YOU CAN DO IT!! KNOCK THE COVER OFF THE BALL!...SEND IT TO MARS!! C'MON, DAD, YOU CAN DO IT!

PING!

BRIAN BASSET

BONK

OH, THANKS FOR COMING TO MY GAME. TOO BAD ABOUT THE CAMERA, THOUGH.

IT'S GOING TO BE A LEAN WEEK UNTIL MY NEXT PAY-CHECK— SO IF YOU COULD PLEASE HOLD OFF FROM BUY-ING ANYTHING UNNECESSARY IT WOULD BE A BIG HELP.

WHAT MAKES YOU THINK I'D DO THAT?
IT'S SOFTBALL SEASON. I KNOW YOU, ADAM. YOU ALWAYS CAN THINK OF SOME-THING NEW TO BUY.
BRIAN BASSET

YEAH, WELL— THE **ONLY** THING I COULD REALLY USE RIGHT NOW WOULD BE A HIGHER BATTING AVERAGE... AND THEY DON'T SELL THOSE.
GOOD!

WAIT A SEC! A **NEW** BAT! YEAH, MAYBE THAT WOULD DO IT?!!

I'M INTERESTED IN A NEW BAT.
SOFTBALL OR HARDBALL?
BATS

SOFTBALL.
ARE YOU A POWER-HITTER OR A SINGLES'-HITTER?
BRIAN BASSET

A SINGLES'-HITTER... I GUESS.
YOU GUESS?

YEAH, I ONLY HAVE A SINGLE HIT ALL SEASON.

NICE BAT, HUH? GUARANTEED TO RAISE YOUR AVERAGE 100 POINTS.
WOW. NO FOOLIN'?
BATS

AND TRIPLE YOUR RBI PRODUCTION! IT'S WORTH ITS WEIGHT IN GOLD.

I'M AFRAID TO ASK. HOW MUCH?
BRIAN BASSET

JUST A MINUTE WHILE I CALL ZURICH FOR TODAY'S GOLD INDEX.

C'MON, ADAM! GET A HIT!!

FOR WHAT MY BOYFRIEND SAYS YOUR HUSBAND PAID FOR THAT NEW BAT HE SHOULD GET PLENTY.
WHAT... DID... HE... PAY?

ADAM! YOU BOUGHT A NEW BAT AFTER I TOLD YOU MONEY WAS TIGHT THIS WEEK!
BRIAN BASSET

YOU'D BETTER NOT GET ONE DING ON THAT BAT! IT'S GOING BACK TO THE STORE!!
STEEERIKE!
SWISH

BRIAN BASSET
TIME, UMP.

LOOK, LAURA. I KNOW MONEY IS TIGHT THIS WEEK, BUT I HAD TO GET A NEW BAT!...ANYTHING TO GET ME OUT OF THIS DREADFUL SLUMP.

OKAY, LET'S SEE THIS MAGIC HUNDRED-DOLLAR BAT DO ITS THING!
THANKS.

AND YOU'D BETTER GET 30 HITS IN A ROW!!!
TALK ABOUT PRESSURE.

BRIAN BASSET
WHAT'RE YOU SUPPOSED TO BE, POOH BEAR?
I'M A LITTLE BLACK RAIN CLOUD, OF COURSE!
C'MON, NICK. THIS IS THE EIGHTH TIME TODAY WE'VE PLAYED THIS VIDEO! COULDN'T WE WATCH ONE OF DADDY'S SHOWS?.. JUST ONCE?
TUT-TUT, IT LOOKS LIKE RAIN.

SILLY O'L BEAR...
BOOP BEEP BOP BEEP
HELLO, GUINNESS BOOK OF WORLD RECORDS?.. I'M NOW WATCHING "WINNIE THE POOH AND THE HONEY TREE" FOR THE NINE HUNDRED. AND FIFTY-THIRD TIME.
BRIAN BASSET

CHEER UP, EEYORE. DON'T BE SO GLOOMY.

NICK! LOOK, OVER THERE!! DO YOU SEE IT?.. THERE, ON THE FAR WALL! WHATEVER YOU DO, DON'T BLINK.... THERE IT GOES AGAIN... KEEP LOOKING!
BRIAN BASSET

CONFOUND IT! WHO TOOK THE BATTERIES OUT OF THE REMOTE CONTROL?!!

ADAM
BY BRIAN BASSET
HEY-- NO BATTA NO BATTA NO BATTA...

CRA

CRACK!

BACK ON THE BALL, ADAM, BACK ON THE BALL! THIS ONE IS REALLY BELTED!!

BRIAN BASSET

ADAM
BY BRIAN BASSET

WHAT A LOUSY MOVIE... WHAT A WASTED EVENING. (SIGH) YOU DON'T THINK WE PUT TOO MUCH IMPORTANCE ON EVERY-THING BEING PERFECT WHEN WE GO OUT SINCE WE DON'T GET OUT MUCH?
I DUNNO. BUT MY CHOCOLATE-COVERED RAISINS WEREN'T CHEWY ENOUGH.
BRIAN BASSET

I'M SORRY, I COULDN'T HEAR YOU... YOU'LL HAVE TO SPEAK LOUDER.

I SAID, "YOU'LL HAVE TO SPEAK LOUDER"!

YOU HAVE TO SPEAK LOUDER!

BRIAN BASSET
HERE. IT'S ALL YOURS.
?
HELLO? HELLO?

WHEN CAREERS AND LIFE STYLES COLLIDE
HUH? WHAT MESS??
BRIAN BASSET

HURRY IT UP, LAURA. THE SITTER SHOULD BE HERE ANY MINUTE!

AHHH, TONIGHT WE TRIP THE LIGHT FANTASTIC!
BRIAN BASSET

CHILD ABANDONER!

TAKE YOUR TIME, LAURA. WE'RE STAYING HOME TONIGHT.

IS THAT THE WASHER 'N' DRYER I HEAR GOING, ADAM?
UH-HUH.
SMOOCH
THAT'S FOR DOING ALL THAT LAUNDRY THAT HAS BEEN PILING UP WITHOUT BEING REMINDED.
ALL THAT LAUNDRY?!
BRIAN BASSET
NO, HECK. IT'S ONLY MY SOFTBALL UNIFORM— I'VE GOT A GAME TONIGHT.
CRACK
BRIAN BASSET
CRASH
COMIC STRIP BORDERS.
GOOD LORD! WHAT HAPPENED TO YOUR FATHER?!
AWW, HE'S OK, MOM. HE KNOCKED HIMSELF OUT FOR A WHILE TRYING TO MAKE A CATCH.
BRIAN BASSET
AND BECAUSE OF THAT, EVERYONE SAID HE WAS THE HERO OF THE GAME!
HIS REPLACEMENT WENT ON TO GET THE GAME-WINNING HIT!

ADAM
BY BRIAN BASSET
JUST ANOTHER 8 DAYS, 22 HOURS, 14 MINUTES AND 36 SECONDS UNTIL THE KIDS GO BACK TO SCHOOL.

35 SECONDS... 34 SECONDS... 33 SECONDS...

AW'RIGHT! 8 MORE DAYS AND THE KIDS ARE BACK IN SCHOOL!
SEPTEMBER

HEY! CAN'T A FATHER GET EXCITED OVER HIS CHILDREN'S EDUCATION?!
BRIAN BASSET

HEY, DAD! THE WATER'S GREAT!! WANNA JOIN US?!
OKAY.

BRILLIANT IDEA, EINSTEIN.
BRIAN BASSET

(SIGH) I WISH WE DIDN'T HAVE TO GO BACK TO SCHOOL NEXT WEEK. DO YOU THINK THERE ARE SOME KIDS SOMEWHERE WHO NEVER HAVE TO GO TO SCHOOL?

SURE! GENIUSES DON'T HAVE TO GO TO SCHOOL.

GOSH, YOU KNOW EVERYTHING, CLAYTON.
BRIAN BASSET

YOU'RE A GENIUS!
YEAH!

IF I AM A GENIUS, AND GENIUSES DON'T HAVE TO GO TO SCHOOL... Y'KNOW WHAT THAT MAKES YOU?...
NO, WHAT?

THE SISTER OF A GENIUS! AND THAT'S ABOUT AS CLOSE TO BEING A GENIUS AS ONE CAN GET.
SO I DON'T HAVE TO GO BACK TO SCHOOL EITHER?!

NO, YOU STILL HAVE TO GO.
BUT ONLY FOR HALF DAYS.
BRIAN BASSET

ADAM
BY BRIAN BASSET
(SIGH) I'M NOT READY FOR SCHOOL TO BEGIN.
ME NEITHER. THE SUMMER WENT BY WAY TOO FAST.

NO. I HAVEN'T DONE ALL MY BACK-TO-SCHOOL SHOPPING.

BRIAN BASSET

AREN'T YOU TWO COMING TO BED?

NAH. WE ONLY HAVE ONE FULL DAY OF SUMMER VACATION LEFT TO SAVOR.
YEAH. WE CAN ALWAYS SLEEP DURING CLASS.

WHAT TIME IS IT, LAURA?
9:30.
BRIAN BASSET

OH, GOOD! THERE'S THIS PROGRAM ON RIGHT NOW THAT SOUNDS REALLY NEAT.
ZAP!

HEY, THAT'S ODD! IT FLIPPED BACK TO THE STATION WE WERE JUST WATCHING.

GOOD LORD!! NOT YOUR VERY OWN CHANNEL CHANGER?!!

ZAP!
BRIAN BASSET

IF YOU ASK ME, THIS IS PRETTY CHILDISH— NOT LETTING ME WATCH WHAT I WANT.
ZAP!

ZAP!

YEAH...WELL, SO WAS GOING OUT AND BUYING YOUR OWN REMOTE CONTROL.

ZAP!

ZAP!

ZAP!

THIS IS CRAZY— CANCELING OUT EACH OTHER'S SHOW! ISN'T THERE SOMETHING ELSE IN THE TV GUIDE WE CAN BOTH AGREE ON?
BRIAN BASSET

WELL... OK.
ZAP!

BY THE WAY, ADAM... THIS IS GREAT FINGER-JELL-O!
IT REALLY IS! THE CONSISTENCY IS PERFECT.
MY LITTLE JASON IS GOBBLING IT UP. I MUST GET THE RECIPE!
SO SEVEN YEARS OF COLLEGE WASN'T A TOTAL WASTE AFTER ALL...
...ADAM NEWMAN... KING OF FINGER-JELL-O.
BRIAN BASSET

PHEW! FINALLY GOT THE KIDS TO BED! WHAT A DAY, WHAT A DAY!
BRIAN BASSET
PLOP!
?
LAURA, WHEN YOU USED TO STAY HOME WITH THE KIDS, DID YOU EVER FEEL, Y'KNOW, UNAPPRECIATED AND INSIGNIFICANT— LIKE WHATEVER YOU DID WAS NEVER SEEN AS BEING ALL THAT IMPORTANT?
WELL, THAT'S HOW I FEEL SOMETIMES.
BRIAN BASSET
THAT'S NICE.

ADAM
BY BRIAN BASSET
GREAT MEAT LOAF LAST NIGHT, DAD!

WHAT DO YOU WANT, CLAYTON?

DAD, CAN YOU TAKE ME TO THE MALL?

HERE. DRIVE YOURSELF.
?

RELAX, LAURA. HE WON'T GET FAR.

I (HEH-HEH) GAVE HIM THE KEY TO MY FILING CABINET.

VRRROOOOM
BRIAN BASSET

ADAM
BY BRIAN BASSET
ARE YOU GOING TO SIT IN FRONT OF THAT TELEVISION ALL DAY?

NO. I GOTTA GO TO BED SOMETIME.

CLICK
HEY.
HEY YOURSELF. YOU SHOULD BE OUTSIDE ON SUCH A NICE DAY LIKE TODAY. C'MON, LET'S TOSS THE FOOTBALL AROUND.

I WANT TO QUARTERBACK FIRST.
SURE, SURE.

OK, GO LONG.
HIKE!

KEEP GOING! THAT'S IT— PAST THE MARTINS' BUICK!

KEEP ON GOING DOWN THE BLOCK!!
FURTHER, FURTHER...
KEEP GOING!!...

BRIAN BASSET

YUP. IT WAS A TOUGH CALL. ONE THAT KEPT ME AWAKE THE LAST FEW NIGHTS. BUT THE WAY I FIGURE IT, WHEN PEOPLE SEE JUST HOW MUCH CANDY IT TAKES TO FILL UP SUCH A LARGE BEAST... WELL... I SHOULD MAKE OUT LIKE A BANDIT.

ADAM
BY BRIAN BASSET
HOW'S YOUR COSTUME COMING?
@*#!!%*

MOM'S SEWING IT RIGHT NOW.

HOW'S CLAYTON'S HALLOWEEN COSTUME COMING?
ALMOST DONE.

BRIAN BASSET

ISN'T THE LOCH NESS MONSTER SUPPOSED TO BE GREEN?

THIS LOCH NESS MONSTER COSTUME SHOULD BRING ME A TON OF CANDY.

WELL.. HOW DO I LOOK?
CAN YOU MOVE ABOUT AND FLAIL YOUR ARMS?
NOT VERY WELL. THIS THING'S PRETTY HEAVY.
THEN YOU LOOK LIKE A GIANT SLUG.
BRIAN BASSET

WAIT UP, GANG! THIS COSTUME'S **HEAVY**.
PANT PANT PANT

PANT PANT

DING DONG
BRIAN BASSET

FORGET THE CANDY. CAN I HAVE A GLASS OF WATER INSTEAD?!
TRICK OR TREAT

BOY, DID I BLOW IT THIS HALLOWEEN. MY DUMB LOCH NESS MONSTER COSTUME WAS SO HEAVY AND AWKWARD THAT I COULD BARELY MOVE.

IT SLOWED ME DOWN SO MUCH THAT MOST HOUSES IN THE NEIGH-BORHOOD HAD RUN OUT OF CANDY LONG BEFORE I COULD HIT MY STRIDE.
BRIAN BASSET
BUT WHAT ***REALLY*** BUGS ME IS THAT I HAVE TO BE NICE TO YOU SO YOU'LL SHARE SOME OF YOUR CANDY WITH ME.
SO I "MIGHT" SHARE SOME OF MY CANDY.

GOLD MINE!
BRIAN BASSET
TRICK OR TREAT

GOLD MINE!

A SHETLAND PONY AND A NEW CAR ON YOUR 18TH BIRTHDAY!
NO! GET YOUR OWN HALLOWEEN CANDY.
BRIAN BASSET

HECTIC DAY, I SEE.
BRIAN BASSET

YEAH. HOW'D YOU KNOW?

YOU ONLY SHAVED HALF YOUR FACE.

ADAM
BY BRIAN BASSET

OK! OK! WE'LL GO TO THE BIG YELLOW "M" FOR LUNCH AS SOON AS WE'RE DONE.

NEXT!

NOT NOW, NICK.

C'MON, CUT IT OUT.

NICK, PLEASE DON'T!

THANK YOU.

BRIAN BASSET
DRIVERS LICENSE RENEWAL PHOTOS
NEXT!

AND WHAT HAVE WE HERE?

15 CENTS MUST'VE FALLEN OUT OF CLAYTON'S PANTS.

HEH-HEH. FINDERS KEEPERS, I ALWAYS SAY.

C'MON. IT'S *ONLY* 15 CENTS!!
BRIAN BASSET

THANKS FOR LOOKING AFTER NICK ON SUCH SHORT NOTICE, LYNN. I REALLY APPRECIATE THIS.
NO PROBLEM, ADAM.
I'LL BE BACK TO PICK HIM UP IN ABOUT THREE HOURS.
GOING TO RUN SOME ERRANDS?
NO, TAKE A NAP.
BRIAN BASSET

DAAAAAD! I'M HOME!

SHHHHHHHHHH— YOU DON'T WANT TO WAKE THE BABY.

THIS IS THE KID WHO'S PAMPERED, CUDDLED, BATHED AND HAND-FED.
BRIAN BASSET

SURE I DO!!

DAD, WHAT'CHA MAKING?
BEEF STEW.

WHY ARE YOU MAKING STEW WHEN CLAYTON SAYS WE'RE HAVING PIZZA FOR DINNER?
BRIAN BASSET

WELL, CLAYTON'S MISTAKEN.
DING DONG!

LARGE PEPPERONI WITH EXTRA CHEESE?...

LOOK WHAT THIS NICE MAN JUST BROUGHT TO OUR DOOR.
PIZZA

CLAYTON! I TOLD YOU I WAS MAKING STEW FOR DINNER.
DING DONG
BRIAN BASSET

SO WHAT DO YOU DO?... YOU GO AND DELIB-ERATELY DEFY ME AND ORDER A PIZZA!

AND WHAT DO YOU WANT?!
MY... MONEY?

TO YOUR ROOM, YOUNG MAN! I WON'T HAVE YOU DELIBERATELY DISOBEYING ME BY ORDERING PIZZAS WHEN YOU KNOW DARN WELL THAT I'VE ALREADY PREPARED SOMETHING ELSE FOR DINNER!

HI, I'M HOME!
BRIAN BASSET

MMMM, PIZZA!!... WHEN DO WE EAT?!

ADAM
BY BRIAN BASSET
I HATE THE HOLIDAY SEASON.

THE HOUSE HAS TO BE KEPT CLEAN FOR COMPANY.

WAIT A SEC! DO I REALLY WANT TO VACUUM THE HOUSE?!
OF COURSE NOT.

AND IS THE CARPET REALLY THAT MESSY??
NAHHHHHHH.

LAURA! THE VACUUM CLEANER JUST DIED!!
CLICK CLICK

GREAT. NOW I KNOW WHAT TO GET YOU FOR CHRISTMAS!
BRIAN BASSET

VRRRRRRRRR

GUESS WHO'S GOING TO BE ON THE RADIO?
YOU, DAD?
WHAT'S ALL THIS ABOUT?
COOL!

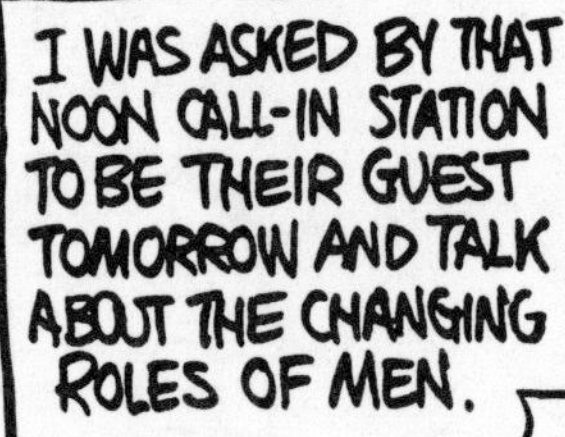
I WAS ASKED BY THAT NOON CALL-IN STATION TO BE THEIR GUEST TOMORROW AND TALK ABOUT THE CHANGING ROLES OF MEN.

TERRIFIC! BUT ISN'T THAT THE PROGRAM PEOPLE CALL WITH THEIR PERSONAL PROBLEMS? HOW'D THEY FIND OUT ABOUT YOU?
BRIAN BASSET

I PHONED IN.

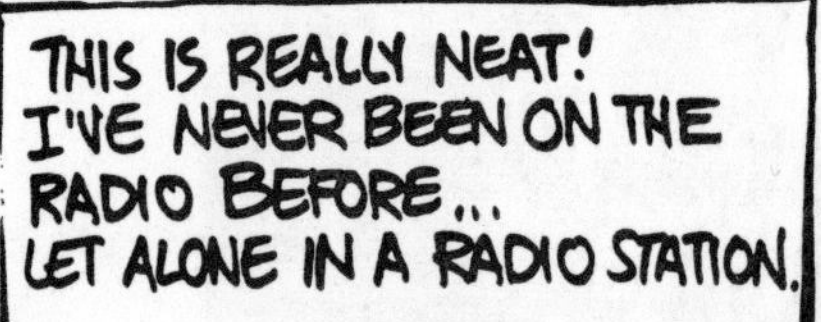
THIS IS REALLY NEAT! I'VE NEVER BEEN ON THE RADIO BEFORE... LET ALONE IN A RADIO STATION.

OF COURSE, MY WIFE WOULD ABSOLUTELY HAVE A COW IF I REALLY SPOKE MY MIND ABOUT STAYING AT HOME.

IN THAT CASE, I'LL PROBABLY JUST TELL SOME FUNNY DIAPERING AND COOKING STORIES THEN. SO— WHEN DO WE GO ON THE AIR?
BRIAN BASSET

WE'RE ON THE AIR.

EARLIER YOU IMPLIED HOW RESENTFUL YOU WERE FOR STAYING HOME WITH THE KIDS. CARE TO ELABORATE ON THAT, MR. NEWMAN?
HUH?!

LOOK, I DIDN'T MEAN TO SAY ANY SUCH THING! OK! NEXT QUESTION.
BRIAN BASSET

SO, WOULD YOU SAY IT'S AN EXTREMELY DEEP-ROOTED RESENTMENT THEN?
YEAH, I GUESS SO.

WE'RE SPEAKING WITH ADAM NEWMAN: HOUSE HUSBAND, FATHER, MODERN MAN EXTRAORDINAIRE. IF YOU HAVE A QUESTION FOR MR. NEWMAN— OUR LINES ARE NOW OPEN.
GO AHEAD. YOU'RE ON THE AIR.

ADAM, WHY DO YOU CONSISTENTLY TOSS 100 PERCENT COTTON ITEMS IN THE DRIER?
GAWD! IT'S MY WIFE!
BRIAN BASSET

BEFORE YOU SAY ANYTHING, LET ME EXPLAIN... Y'SEE, I-I DIDN'T REALLY MEAN TO SAY I WAS RESENTFUL FOR STAYING HOME WITH THE KIDS...

IT'S JUST THAT... WELL, I'D NEVER BEEN ON THE RADIO BEFORE AND I WAS, Y'KNOW, KIND OF NERVOUS THAT I MIGHT SAY SOMETHING DUMB.
BRIAN BASSET

I DON'T THINK YOU HAVE ANYTHING TO WORRY ABOUT.
REALLY? I DIDN'T SAY ANYTHING DUMB?
NO, YOU DIDN'T SOUND NERVOUS.

THE YEAR BEFORE THAT I ASKED FOR AN ANTI-TANK MISSILE LAUNCHER WITH AN INFRARED SCOPE— AND HE BRINGS ME AN ANT FARM.

WHAT'RE YOU GIVING LAURA FOR CHRISTMAS, ADAM?
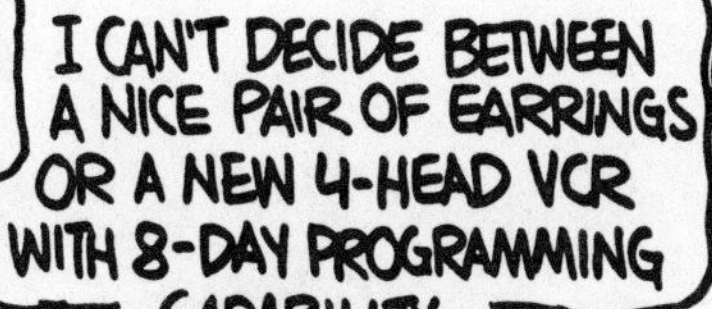
I CAN'T DECIDE BETWEEN A NICE PAIR OF EARRINGS OR A NEW 4-HEAD VCR WITH 8-DAY PROGRAMMING CAPABILITY.

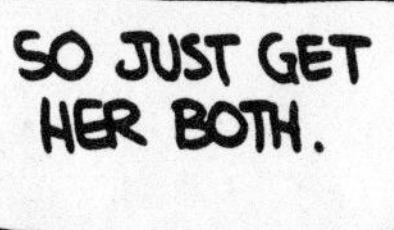
SO JUST GET HER BOTH.

BRIAN BASSET

WHY? I DON'T WEAR EARRINGS.

MAY I HELP YOU?
YES. I'M LOOKING FOR A NIGHTGOWN FOR MY WIFE.

SOMETHING SORT OF SEXY AND LACY... BUT PRACTICAL.
BRIAN BASSET
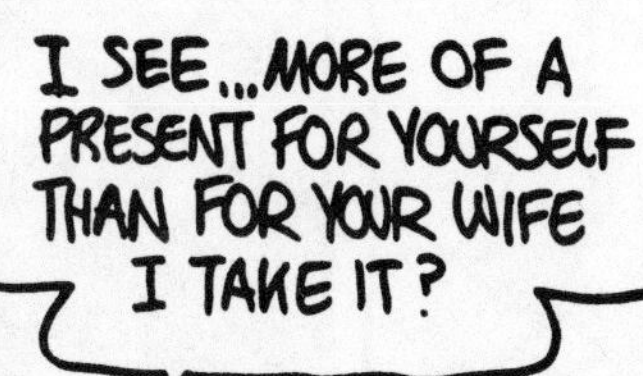
I SEE... MORE OF A PRESENT FOR YOURSELF THAN FOR YOUR WIFE I TAKE IT?

LADY! I MAY STAY HOME WITH THE KIDS AND DO THE COOKING AND CLEANING AND STUFF, BUT THAT'S AS FAR AS IT GOES!

DADDY, WHAT'RE THOSE GREEN THINGS IN THE FRUITCAKE CALLED?
NOT NOW, KATY... I'M BUSY. ASK YOUR MOM.

BRIAN BASSET

SO, WHAT ARE THOSE GREEN THINGS IN THE FRUITCAKE CALLED?

ADAM
BY BRIAN BASSET
ATTENTION SHOPPERS!

JUST 104 SHOPPING DAYS TILL EASTER!

CAN'T FIND YOUR WIFE IN THAT MAZE EITHER, EH?

NO, THIS IS HOW I CHRISTMAS SHOP.

ADAM
BY BRIAN BASSET
LAURA, WHERE'S THE WRAPPING PAPER AND TAPE?!
WHERE WE'VE ALWAYS KEPT IT.

WHERE'S THAT?!

BRIAN BASSET

OH WELL, THE CHILDREN WERE STARTING TO SHOW SIGNS OF NOT BELIEVING IN SANTA, ANYWAY.

DAD, CAN I HAVE SECONDS?...PLEASE!

WELL, OF COURSE YOU CAN! AND TO THINK I THOUGHT YOU WEREN'T GOING TO LIKE WHAT I FIXED TONIGHT.
BRIAN BASSET

'TIS THE SEASON TO GIVE, Y'KNOW.
?
?

OHHH (HEH-HEE), HE MUST MEAN AS IN GIVING OUT "COMPLIMENTS."

MERRY CHRISTMAS!
MERRY CHRISTMAS!
MERRY CHRISTMAS!
SOME ASSEMBLY REQUIRED... SOME ASSEMBLY REQUIRED... SOME ASSEMBLY REQUIRED....
BRIAN BASSET

THERE! IT'S NOT CROOKED ANYMORE!
THAT'S BECAUSE IT'S HORIZONTAL.

ADAM
BY BRIAN BASSET
YOU LOOK SO DANG SWEET IN THAT PARTY HAT, ADAM.

LIKE A BIG UPSIDE-DOWN ICE CREAM CONE.

THUMP!

WHOA! DON'T YOU THINK WE'RE JUMPING THE GUN A BIT?— IT ISN'T THE NEW YEAR YET.

IT IS SOMEWHERE!
BRIAN BASSET

BRIAN BASSET
I HOPE YOU'RE NOT GOING TO LIE THERE ALL DAY WATCHING NOTHING BUT BOWL GAMES, ADAM ?!
OF COURSE NOT.

THAT'S GOOD TO HEAR.
THERE ARE THE COMMERCIALS, TOO.

MAKE ANY NEW YEAR'S RESOLUTIONS, LAURA?
MMM- JUST ONE.

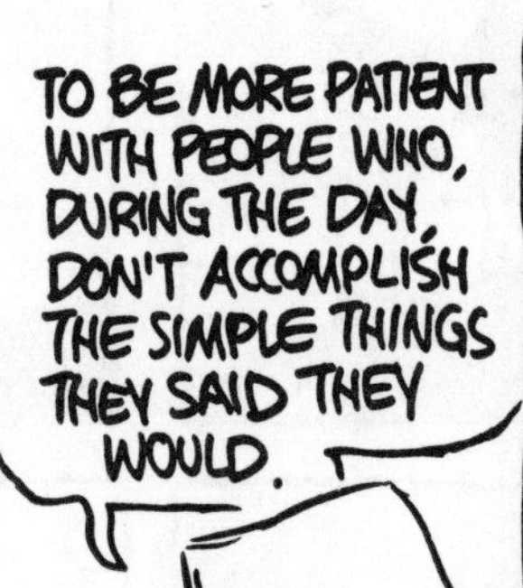
TO BE MORE PATIENT WITH PEOPLE WHO, DURING THE DAY, DON'T ACCOMPLISH THE SIMPLE THINGS THEY SAID THEY WOULD.

GEE, I DIDN'T REALIZE HOW FRUSTRATING THINGS MUST BE FOR YOU DOWN AT THE OFFICE.
BRIAN BASSET

I'M ***NOT*** TALKING ABOUT THE OFFICE.

SO, DID YOU MAKE ANY NEW YEAR'S RESOLUTIONS, CLAYTON?
WHAT'RE THOSE?

Y'KNOW, LIKE TURNING C'S INTO B'S AND B'S INTO A'S.

BUT ***THAT'S*** CHEATING.
BRIAN BASSET

NO! BY STUDYING ***HARDER***!
OHHH.

ADAM
BY BRIAN BASSET

HEY, NO FAIR! I (PANT-PANT) ATE MORE THAN YOU OVER THE HOLIDAYS!

LOOK, NICK! IF YOU WANNA GO OUTSIDE YOU NEED TO WEAR A COAT... IT'S FREEZING OUT THERE!

BRIAN BASSET

I DID IT, LAURA! I JOINED A HEALTH CLUB TODAY.

THAT WAS QUICK. I THOUGHT YOU WERE GOING TO RESEARCH THIS CAREFULLY.
AND I DID!

YOU FOUND ONE THAT'S WITHIN OUR BUDGET? ONE THAT'S CONVENIENT? ONE THAT HAS WEIGHTS, A POOL AND AEROBICS LIKE YOU SAID YOU WANTED?

EVEN BETTER! I FOUND ONE WITH *BABY-SITTING!*
BRIAN BASSET

BEFORE WE START YOUR PROGRAM, WE NEED TO GET YOUR MEASUREMENTS SO WE CAN CHART YOUR PROGRESS.

WAIST, 41 INCHES.
41 INCHES?? ARE YOU SURE? THAT SEEMS A BIT OFF.

YOU COULD BE RIGHT. HOLD ON.
YUP! 43 INCHES.
BRIAN BASSET

THAT SEEMS LIKE AN AWFUL LOT OF WEIGHT TO START WITH.
NAHHHH.

OK, GIVE IT A TRY, AND I'LL BE RIGHT BACK.

BRIAN BASSET
CRACK

WELL, HOW'D HE DO?

HE ONLY CRIED FOR A FEW MINUTES AFTER YOU LEFT.
BRIAN BASSET

THAT'S GOOD TO HEAR!

THE REST OF THE TIME HE THREW THINGS AND KICKED THE OTHER KIDS.

WELL, HOW'D YOUR FIRST WORKOUT GO TODAY, ADAM?

I'M SORE FROM HEAD TO TOE.
BRIAN BASSET

AND HOW'D THE CLUB'S DAY CARE WORK OUT WITH NICK?

THEY OFFERED ME DOUBLE MY MONEY BACK IF I'D TAKE MY MEMBERSHIP ELSEWHERE.

DAD, NOW THAT YOU'VE BEEN WORKING OUT— COULD I FEEL YOUR MUSCLE?
(HEH-HEH) SURE.

WOW!
KIDS!

SAY, DAD?..
UH-HUH.
BRIAN BASSET

IF I GAVE YOU THE NAME OF THIS BULLY AT SCHOOL, WOULD YOU BEAT HIM UP FOR ME?

CLAYTON, I ONLY HOPE YOU WERE JOKING WHEN YOU ASKED ME TO BEAT UP SOME BULLY AT SCHOOL FOR YOU!

OH, I **WAS**.
WELL, **GOOD**!

DAD?...
YES.
BRIAN BASSET

WOULD YOU GO **12** ROUNDS WITH HIS DAD?

PSSST, CLAYTON. WHY'D YOU GET SENT TO YOUR ROOM?
I ASKED DAD TO BEAT UP THIS BULLY AT SCHOOL'S DAD.

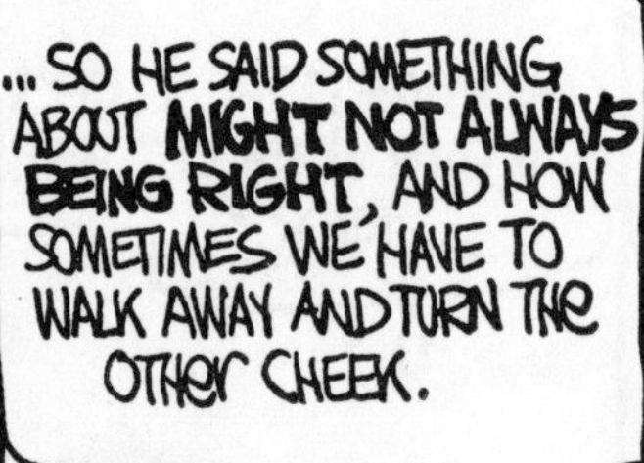
...SO HE SAID SOMETHING ABOUT **MIGHT NOT ALWAYS BEING RIGHT**, AND HOW SOMETIMES WE HAVE TO WALK AWAY AND TURN THE OTHER CHEEK.

AND ***THEN*** YOU GOT SENT UPSTAIRS?
NO.
BRIAN BASSET

IT WAS AFTER I CALLED HIM "CHICKEN."

LAURA, TAKE A LOOK AT **THIS**. ***NOT*** BAD FOR ONLY A FEW WEEKS AT THE GYM.

YOU'RE SUCKING YOUR STOMACH IN, ADAM!
BRIAN BASSET

OK, OK, BUT I WAS ***NEVER*** ABLE TO HOLD IT THAT LONG BEFORE I STARTED WORKING OUT!

ADAM
BY BRIAN BASSET

BONK!

TWO!

THREE!

FOUR!

BRIAN BASSET

105!

106!

SEVEN!..

CLUB
DAYCARE

CLUB
DAYCARE
BRIAN BASSET

CLUB
DAYCARE

WAHAHHH
DON'T DO THIS TO ME! DON'T LEAVE ME WITH **THIS** KID!!
CLUB
DAYCARE

DID YOU WORK OUT TODAY?
UH-HUH!

AND HOW'S NICK TAKING TO THE CLUB'S DAYCARE?
WELL... LEM'ME SEE— HE ONLY SCREAMED FOR 20 MINUTES THIS TIME.
BRIAN BASSET

AT LEAST HE'S IMPROVING. HOW LONG DID YOU WORK OUT?
20 MINUTES.

HEY, DAD, CAN I HAVE A RAISE IN MY ALLOWANCE?
WHEN YOU START KEEPING YOUR ROOM TIDY LIKE WE TALKED ABOUT.

WELL... HOW 'BOUT IF YOU JUST GIVE ME A RAISE ***NOT*** TO MAKE IT ANY MORE OF A MESS?
THAT'S EXTORTION!
BRIAN BASSET

C'MON, ADAM— HARDER, HARDER! YOU CAN DO IT! THAT'S IT... PUSH IT TO THE MAX!!
BARB

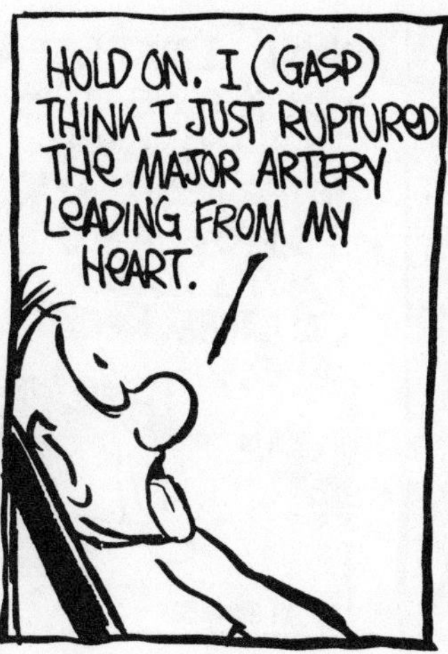
HOLD ON. I (GASP) THINK I JUST RUPTURED THE MAJOR ARTERY LEADING FROM MY HEART.

BRIAN BASSET
NO PAIN, NO GAIN.

STAIRMASTER SIGN UP

ALMOST DONE?

NO, I JUST STARTED.

BRIAN BASSET

I'M HOME
BRIAN BASSET

? ? ?

LAURA— THERE WAS NOTHING CLEAN TO EAT OFF OF SO I TOOK THE KIDS OUT TO DINNER. —ADAM

P.S. FEEL FREE TO DO THE DISHES.

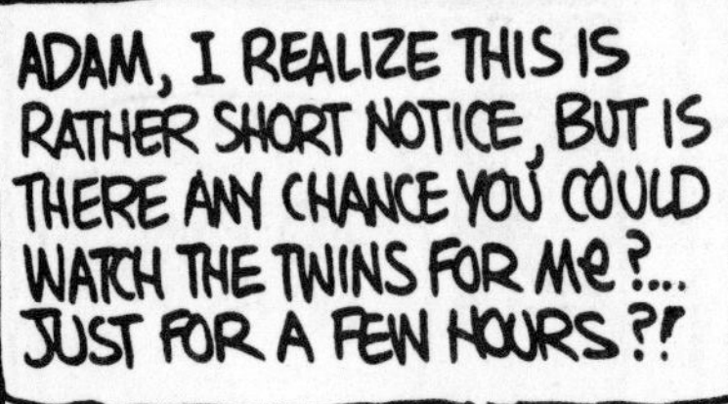
ADAM, I REALIZE THIS IS RATHER SHORT NOTICE, BUT IS THERE ANY CHANCE YOU COULD WATCH THE TWINS FOR ME?... JUST FOR A FEW HOURS?!

Y'SEE, I JUST GOT A CALL TO COME DOWN-TOWN FOR A JOB INTERVIEW!! NOW, I SUPPOSE IF YOU CAN'T I COULD CALL THEM BACK AND...
BRIAN BASSET
CAROL, I'D REALLY LIKE TO, BUT...
I'LL PAY YOU FOUR DOLLARS AN HOUR!
PSSST, G'WAN, TAKE IT. THAT'S MORE THAN YOU MADE ALL LAST YEAR!
OK!

BRIAN BASSET
HEY! WHO TOOK THE TOILET PAPER?!!

ADAM! LOOK AT THIS PLACE... IT'S A DISASTER! TOYS SCATTERED EVERY-WHERE... CLOTHES STREWN ALL ABOUT.
I DON'T MEAN TO SOUND NEGATIVE, BUT DON'T YOU EVER PICK ANYTHING UP?
SURE, BUT YOU KNOW HOW KIDS ARE...
THEY MAKE A MESS— I PICK IT UP. THEY MAKE A MESS AGAIN— I PICK IT UP. THEY MAKE ANOTHER MESS— I PICK THAT UP... AND SO ON AND SO FORTH.
YES?! SO WHY DIDN'T YOU PICK THIS ONE UP?
HEY, IT WOULDN'T BE FAIR IF I DIDN'T LET THEM WIN EVERY NOW AND THEN.
BRIAN BASSET

PSST, LAURA...NICK'S CRYING... YOUR TURN TO GET UP WITH HIM.
HUH? MINE?? I GOT UP WITH HIM YESTERDAY.

YEAH, OK...BUT THERE'S NO SENSE IN MY GETTING OUT OF BED—— YOU'RE THE ONE WHO SAYS YOU CAN NEVER FALL BACK ASLEEP AFTER WAKING UP.
SO YOU MIGHT AS WELL GET UP WITH HIM.
BRIAN BASSET

JUST COME UP AND WAKE ME WHEN YOU NEED TO GET READY FOR WORK.
FINE! I THINK I'LL GO IN EARLY THIS MORNING.

GREAT LUNCH TODAY, DAD!

I WAS ABLE TO GET HALF A PEANUT BUTTER 'N' JELLY ON WHITE AND AN APPLE FOR IT.
BRIAN BASSET

CLAYTON, YOU KNOW HOW I FEEL ABOUT TRADING WHAT I'VE FIXED YOU.
OH, AND BEST OF ALL—— A SLICE OF BOSTON CREAM PIE!

REALLY? ME? I WAS WORTH BOSTON CREAM PIE??...WOW!
YEAH! A REALLY BIG PIECE, TOO!

SO, WHAT ELSE DID YOU DO TODAY, ADAM?

I CHANGED 6,000 POOPY DIAPERS.
BRIAN BASSET

OH REALLY? AND DID YOU GIVE THE FOLKS AT THE GUINNESS BOOK OF WORLD RECORDS A CALL?

DIDN'T HAVE TIME. I WAS CHANGING DIAPERS.

PUT NICK DOWN AT 7:30, AND CLAYTON AND KATY SHOULD BE IN BED NO LATER THAN 8:30.

AW'RIGHT, LET'S BOOGIE! I'VE BEEN DYING TO SEE THIS MOVIE!
(YAWN) ME TOO.

ADAM, YOU LOOK POSITIVELY EXHAUSTED. WE COULD JUST STAY HOME, Y'KNOW.

ARE YOU CRAZY?! STAYING HOME IS THE REASON I'M EXHAUSTED!

I'M GOING TO GET SOME POPCORN BEFORE THE MOVIE STARTS. WANT ANYTHING?
STRONG COFFEE.

BRIAN BASSET
NEXT.
POP CORN

TERRIFIC. NOW WHAT ROW ARE WE IN?
POP CORN

BINGO!
Z

POP CORN
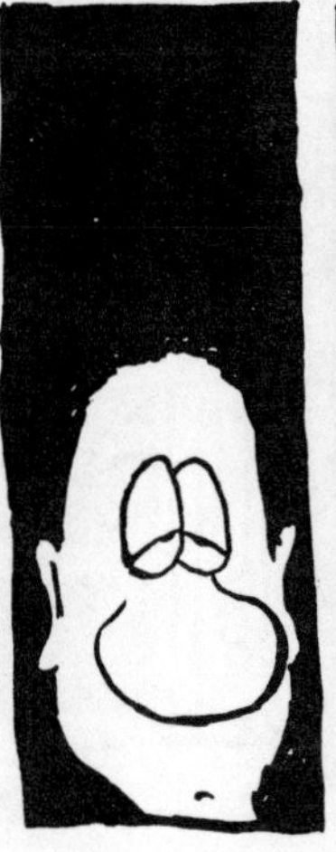
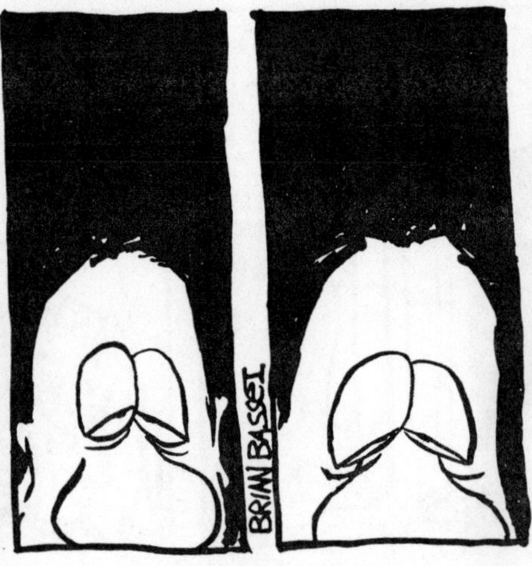
BRIAN BASSET

HEY, DOWN IN FRONT!! WE CAN'T SEE!!
Z

ADAM
BY BRIAN BASSET

LAURA.

I WANT A CHANGE.

JUST LIKE THAT? YOU WANT A CHANGE?
UH-HUH.

ADAM, WE AGREED WE'D STICK WITH THIS FOR A WHILE. DON'T THINK FOR ONE MINUTE THAT YOUR STAYING AT HOME WITH THE KIDS HASN'T BEEN HARD ON ME, TOO!

BUSINESS TRIPS THAT TAKE ME FAR AWAY FROM THE FAMILY... GUILT TRIPS YOU LAY ON ME... THE PRESSURE OF PROVIDING FOR EVERYONE!

THIS HAS NOTHING TO DO WITH MY STAYING AT HOME!

GREAT! YOU FOUND SOMEONE YOUNGER AND MORE ATTRACTIVE! I SHOULD'VE KNOWN!!
BRIAN BASSET

AND ALL I WANTED WAS TO CHANGE THE CHANNEL.

ADAM
BY BRIAN BASSET

G'WAN, ADAM! HOW WILL YOU EVER KNOW IF YOU'RE AN EXPERT SKIER IF YOU NEVER SKI THE EXPERT SLOPES?!

AAAAAAAAAAAAAAAA

WE'LL NEED A LADDER, A CHAIN SAW...
BRIAN BASSET

ADAM
BY BRIAN BASSET
MOM, CAN I SEE THE PAPER WHEN YOU'RE DONE WITH IT?

WHAT SECTION? THE COMICS?
NO, THE HORSE RACING RESULTS.

MMMM, GOOD COFFEE THIS MORNING, ADAM.
THANK YOU.

WAIT A SEC! SHOULDN'T YOU REALLY BE THANKING ALL THE PEASANTS WHO TOIL FOR MEAGER WAGES PICKING EVERY BEAN BY HAND?

I NEVER THOUGHT OF IT LIKE THAT.
AND THEN THERE ARE THE PEOPLE WHO SHIP IT, ROAST IT, PACKAGE IT...

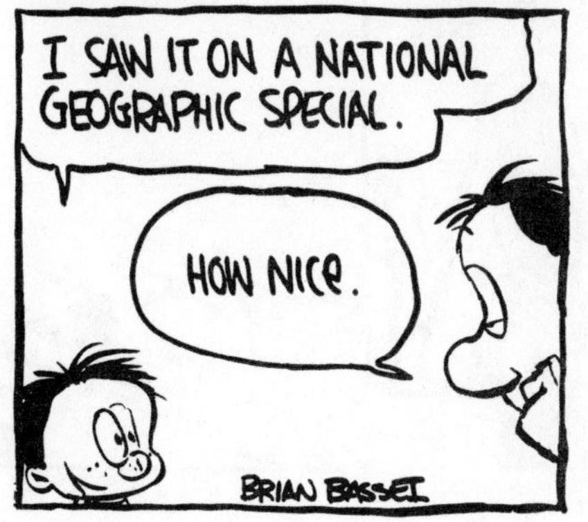
I SAW IT ON A NATIONAL GEOGRAPHIC SPECIAL.
HOW NICE.
BRIAN BASSET

MMMMM, GOOD EGGS, ADAM.
THANK YOU.
WAIT A SEC!...

NO UMBRELLAS?? IT'S POURING OUT THERE!
TEENAGE MUTANT NINJA TURTLES DON'T NEED UMBRELLAS!

BRIAN BASSET

TEENAGE MUTANT NINJA TURTLES... HEROES IN A HALF SHELL!...
...TURTLE POWER!

BRIAN BASSET

?

?
KIP

I TOLD YOU... NO COOKIES THIS CLOSE TO DINNER-TIME!

HEY, I THOUGHT YOU TEENAGE MUTANT NINJA TURTLES ALWAYS RAN IN PACKS OF FOUR.

BRIAN BASSET

WHERE ARE THE KIDS??
THE KIDS?

READY FOR A SHOCK?...
SOMETHING'S HAPPENED TO THEM?! WHAT? WHAT?!
THEY'VE... THEY'VE TURNED INTO TEENAGE MUTANT NINJA TURTLES.
OH, THANK GOD!
BRIAN BASSET

CLAYTON, QUIT PLAYING WITH YOUR MEAT LOAF!

TEENAGE MUTANT NINJA TURTLES DON'T EAT SLOP LIKE THIS! WE ONLY LIKE PIZZA!
CLAYTON!
BRIAN BASSET

OF COURSE, SINCE WE DO COME FROM SEWERS, I SUPPOSE WE CAN EAT JUST ABOUT ANYTHING.
CLAYTON!

I JUST DON'T KNOW HOW I FEEL ABOUT THIS MUTANT TURTLE NINJA TEENAGER STUFF.
TEENAGE MUTANT NINJA TURTLES.

AWWWW, LAURA...IT'S ONLY A PHASE THE KIDS ARE GOING THROUGH.
BRIAN BASSET

YES, BUT IT SEEMS SO VIOLENT.

WHATEVER HAPPENED TO COWBOYS AND INDIANS?!

RINGG
HELLO?... WHAT'S THAT YOU SAY?... MY SON DONATELLO HAS BEEN SCARING THE OTHER CHILDREN AT RECESS WITH HIS TEENAGE MUTANT NINJA TURTLE STICKS?

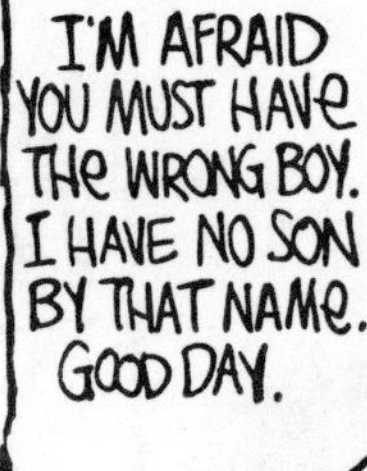
I'M AFRAID YOU MUST HAVE THE WRONG BOY. I HAVE NO SON BY THAT NAME. GOOD DAY.

BRIAN BASSET

HI, I'M HERE TO PICK UP MY SON, CLAYTON.
PRINCIPAL'S OFFICE
WE HAVE NO ONE BY THAT NAME.

YOU DON'T? BUT I JUST GOT A PHONE CALL SAYING TO COME GET HIM... THAT HE'D BEEN SENT DOWN HERE.

SORRY. THERE'S NO CLAYTON HERE.

BRIAN BASSET

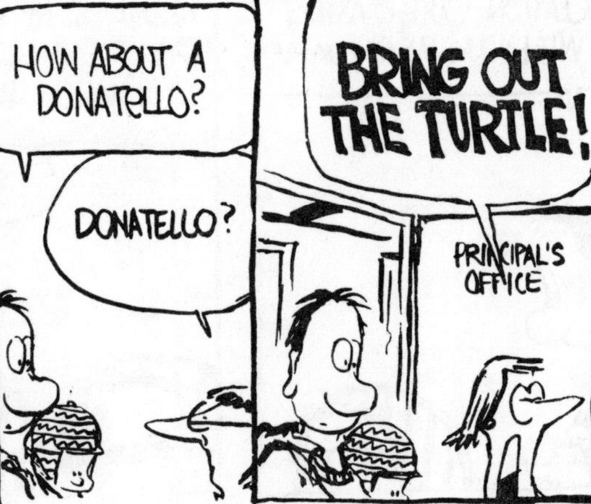
HOW ABOUT A DONATELLO?
DONATELLO?
BRING OUT THE TURTLE!
PRINCIPAL'S OFFICE

CLAYTON! YOU JUST CAN'T PRETEND TO BE A TEENAGE MUTANT NINJA TURTLE AND GO AROUND SCARING THE OTHER KIDS AT SCHOOL!

I WASN'T JUST ANY TURTLE! I WAS DONATELLO!
WHATEVER. JUST DON'T DO IT AGAIN!
BRIAN BASSET
YES SIR.

BUT WHAT IF THEY'RE SHREDDER AND ROCKSTEADY, AND THEY HAVE SOME EVIL PLAN TO FOUL UP THE CITY'S WATER SUPPLY, AND...
YOUR MOTHER CAN HANDLE THIS ONE.

YOUR MOTHER AND I HAVE DECIDED THAT IF THE TWO OF YOU WILL STOP PRETENDING TO BE MUTANT NINJA TURTLES, THEN WE'LL BUY YOU THE ENTIRE NINJA TURTLE COLLECTION.

BRIAN BASSET
WELL...
I GUESS THAT'S OK.
SEE? I TOLD YOU IT WOULD WORK.

SEE? I TOLD YOU IT WOULD WORK.

I WANT THAT ONE! SHREDDER, EVIL LORD OF DESTRUCTION!
NO, I ONLY WANT YOU TO HAVE A GOOD GUY.

WAHHHH HHHH
I WANT THAT ONE!
BRIAN BASSET

WELL, UH... IS HE A GOOD BAD-GUY?!
YEAH (SNIFF)
OK, OK! JUST GET IT AND LET'S GO!

I WANT THAT ONE!

PHEW! ONLY TWO TEENAGE MUTANT NINJA TURTLES LEFT!
TURTLES

OUT OF THE WAY! I SAW THEM FIRST!!
WUMP!

FORGET IT LADY, I DID!
NO, I DID!
A GOOD GUY! I'VE GOT TO HAVE THAT ONE!
BRIAN BASSET

A GOOD GUY? WHERE? WHERE?
HEY (OOF) QUIT SHOVING!
BACK OFF LADY!!
I WASN'T YOU BIG FA
AND THEY'RE AFRAID NINJA TURTLES WILL MAKE US AGGRESSIVE??

ADAM
BY BRIAN BASSET
AWWWW, NICK. DID YOU THINK DADDY WASN'T COMING BACK FOR YOU?
SNIFF

HE WASN'T THE ONE WHO WAS WORRIED.

THANKS FOR WATCHING NICK FOR ME, LYNN. I HOPE HE WASN'T ANY TROUBLE.
NOT IN THE LEAST. THE BOYS PLAYED BEAUTIFULLY TOGETHER.

THAT'S GOOD TO HEAR! OH, WHEN DID YOU WANT TO DROP COLE OFF AT MY PLACE NEXT?
WEDNESDAY AT 9:30, OK?
BRIAN BASSET

GREAT! WE'LL SEE HIM THEN!

THE LITTLE TERROR.
GEEESH! I THOUGHT HE'D NEVER COME FOR THAT MONSTER.

ADAM
BY BRIAN BASSET
SECONDS, ADAM?
SURE— WHY NOT.

...I'VE ALREADY HAD FOURTHS.

DELICIOUS POPPY SEED CAKE, CONNIE.
THANKS. I FOUND THE RECIPE IN AN OLD MAGAZINE LAST MONTH.

SCRUMPTIOUS! I'LL BRING A COFFEE CAKE OR SOMETHING NEXT WEEK.
BUT YOU BROUGHT A PUMPKIN BREAD LAST WEEK.
RIGHT. IT'S KIM'S TURN NEXT WEEK.

THEN MINE, 'CAUSE I REMEMBER BRINGING DOUGHNUT-HOLES THE WEEK AFTER SHE BROUGHT CINNAMON ROLLS.
THAT'S RIGHT.

DOCTOR'S OFFICE
SPEAKING OF KIM, HERE SHE IS WITH CHRISTOPHER.
MR. NEWMAN, THE DOCTOR WILL SEE NICK NOW.
HACK WHEEEZ COUGH
HACK COUGH HACK
AHH-CHOOO
BRIAN BASSET

MY DAD'S BIGGER THAN YOUR DAD! MY DAD'S STRONGER THAN YOUR DAD!

AND MY DAD MAKES MORE MONEY THAN YOUR DAD!

OH, YEAH? WELL, UH... MY DAD PAYS LESS TAXES THAN YOUR DAD!

BRIAN BASSET

HOW WAS, ER... BASKETBALL THIS EVENING, ADAM?
THAT DENNIS GETS ME SO MAD SOMETIMES!
SLAM!

WHAT? I SUPPOSE HE'S LIKE ALL THE OTHER GUYS AND DOESN'T PASS YOU THE BALL ENOUGH?
BRIAN BASSET

NO, THAT'S NOT IT.

HIS SON'S POTTY-TRAINED ALREADY!

HEY, DENNIS, THIS IS ADAM. Y'KNOW HOW YOU SAID YOUR SON IS NOW POTTY-TRAINED—— WELL, GUESS WHAT?!

NO, NO, NICK ISN'T POTTY-TRAINED. NO, SOMETHING ALMOST BETTER... GIVE UP? OK, OUR BABYSITTER JUST GOT HER DRIVER'S LICENSE! WE DON'T HAVE TO PICK HER UP ANYMORE!

OH.
BRIAN BASSET

HE SAID HIS MOTHER-IN-LAW HAS BEEN DRIVING FOR YEARS, AND SHE WATCHES BEN FOR FREE.

ADAM
BY BRIAN BASSET
I HATE RAINY DAYS.

...THEY REMIND ME OF BATH TIME.

RAIN, RAIN, GO AWAY COME AGAIN ANOTHER DAY!

HEY! IT STOPPED RAINING!

BRIAN BASSET

SISTER, SISTER, GO AWAY BE A PEST ANOTHER DAY!
?

MOMMY! DADDY!

WOW! IT REALLY WORKS.

ADAM
BY BRIAN BASSET
SNIFF
SNIFF

ADAM MUST BE HOME.

YOU'RE BACK! HOW WAS BASKETBALL THIS MORNING?
OK. OUR SIDE WON FIVE OF SEVEN.

YOU DON'T SOUND TOO THRILLED.

OH... IN THE LAST GAME I WAS CLOSING IN ON SCORING THE 2,000TH POINT OF MY CAREER!

THAT WAS UNTIL JEFF STARTED HOGGING THE BALL! SO NOW I HAVE TO WAIT ANOTHER WEEK.
BRIAN BASSET

PLOP

?

I DIDN'T KNOW THEY KEPT THOSE KIND OF RECORDS FOR PICK-UP GAMES.
THEY DON'T.

..I DO.

MAN, JUST LISTEN TO THAT KID SCREAM. HE MUST REALLY HATE BEING PUT IN THE CLUB'S DAY-CARE.
WAHHHHHH
WAH
I GOTTA ADMIT—THAT'S QUITE A SET OF LUNGS HE HAS.
YEAH, WELL, IT DOESN'T SEEM TO PUT A DAMPER ON YOUR WORKOUT.

BRIAN BASSET
HEY, SO YOU'RE THE ONE SELLING HEADPHONES!! HOW MUCH?!
WAHHHHHHHHHHHH

ARRGGHHHH
OOOOMPHH
GRUNT-UMPH-GRUNT

WELL (PANT-PANT), HOW WAS THAT, BARB?
BRIAN BASSET

NOT BAD. YOUR ARRGGHHHH SOUNDS GOOD. YOU'VE COME UP ON YOUR OOOOMPHH... BUT YOUR GRUNT-UMPH-GRUNT COULD USE SOME WORK.

...AND IF THESE PROJECTIONS ARE ACCURATE, THEN WE CAN EXPECT TO SEE SIGNIFICANT GAINS IN...
er, excuse me MRS. NEWMAN...

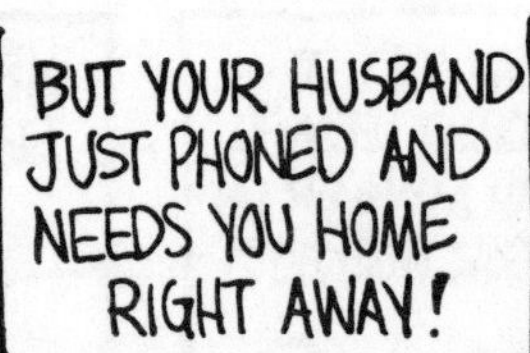
BUT YOUR HUSBAND JUST PHONED AND NEEDS YOU HOME RIGHT AWAY!

BRIAN BASSET

DID HE SAY WHY?
Yes, MA'AM. HE SAID HE THREW HIS BACK OUT TRYING TO PICK UP THE BABY AND IS NOW LYING FLAT ON THE FLOOR.

PLUS, SOMETHING ABOUT NOT BEING ABLE TO REACH THE CHANNEL CHANGER.

WHAT'CHA DOING ON THE FLOOR, DAD?
THANK GOD YOU'RE HOME! I THREW MY BACK OUT. WHAT'S NICK UP TO?

HE'S ON THE COUCH WATCHING SESAME STREET.
HI, DADDY.
HI, PRINCESS.

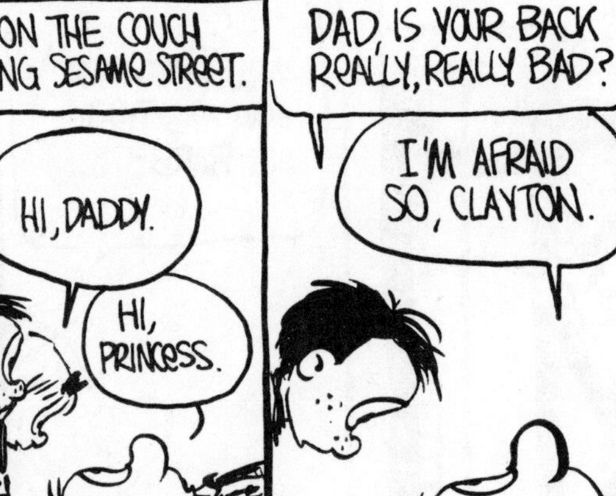
DAD, IS YOUR BACK REALLY, REALLY BAD?
I'M AFRAID SO, CLAYTON.

BRIAN BASSET
AW'RIGHT! WE CAN ORDER A PIZZA FOR DINNER!
AWESOME

TRIP!

I NOTICE ON THE CALENDAR THAT YOU HAVE YOUR MOTHER/BABY GROUP THIS MORNING AT 9:30, ADAM.
APRIL
BRIAN BASSET
OH MY GOSH, I FORGOT! IT'S NOT HERE, IS IT?!
NO, IT'S AT LYNN'S.
PHEW! I SHOULD HAVE JUST ENOUGH TIME TO GET NICK AND ME READY.
AND YOU'VE MARKED DOWN THAT YOU'RE SUPPOSED TO BRING THE BAKED GOODS.
GOOD LORD— I'M SUPPOSED TO BRING THE SNACK FOR THE MOTHER/BABY GROUP THIS MORNING, AND THE REFRIGERATOR'S PRACTICALLY BARE!
AND SO ARE THE CUPBOARDS!!
BRIAN BASSET
WHAT AM I GOING TO DO?! I'VE GOT LESS THAN 12 MINUTES TO COME UP WITH SOMETHING HALFWAY EDIBLE!
WELL, IF **NECESSITY** IS THE MOTHER OF INVENTION... ***THEN* DESPERATION** WILL HAVE TO BE THE FATHER OF BRAN FLAKES AND VANILLA-EXTRACT STICKY-BALL CLUSTERS.
CORN SYRUP
I HOPE NO ONE'S HOME. I HOPE NO ONE'S HOME. I HOPE NO ONE'S HOME. I HOPE...
BZZZZZ
HI, LYNN. I HOPE I'M NOT TOO LATE?
MAYBE A LITTLE, BUT THAT'S OK.
...EVERYONE'S EAGERLY AWAITING THE GOODIES YOU BAKED.
BRIAN BASSET
PSSST. TAKE A LOOK AT THAT GUILTY SMIRK ON ADAM'S FACE. I'LL BET LAURA ACTUALLY MADE IT.
THAT OR HE STOPPED AT THE BAKERY.

MMMM, THIS LOOKS QUITE INTERESTING, ADAM.
RATHER GOOEY. IT MUST BE SINFUL!
TELL US THE TRUTH. DID LAURA MAKE IT?
MMFFPHRMMBBRFF MMFFPMMHHBRRMF MMPHPPFFM MPRMUPFF MPHHM
YES! LAURA MADE IT!!
BRIAN BASSET

HI, HOW WAS YOUR DAY?
FINE.
WERE YOU ABLE TO PICK UP SOMETHING AT THE BAKERY TO TAKE FOR YOUR MOTHER/BABY GROUP?
DIDN'T HAVE TIME. SO I THREW SOMETHING TOGETHER REALLY FAST.
ER... INTERESTING LOOKING DINNER, ADAM. UM... WHERE'D IT COME FROM?
THE MOTHER/BABY GROUP.
BRIAN BASSET

OPE
PARENTING
THE PEACE CORPS
THE TOUGHEST JOB YOU'LL EVER LOVE
BRIAN BASSET

..AND I'LL HAVE ONE KID'S HAPPY-PACK MEAL THAT COMES WITH THE THREE-HEADED SHARK MONSTER FROM THE ZARGON GALAXY.
I'M SORRY, SIR. WE'RE NO LONGER GIVING OUT THAT TOY.

YOU'VE GOT TO HAVE THAT ONE! MY SON HERE NEEDS IT FOR HIS COLLECTION! I WAS HERE THE OTHER DAY AND YOU HADN'T STARTED HANDING IT OUT YET!

YES, WELL, IT WAS VERY POPULAR, SIR, AND WE RAN OUT EARLY. PERHAPS YOUR SON WOULD LIKE A SMURF ON ROLLER SKATES INSTEAD.
BRIAN BASSET

GIVE ME A BREAK! WHAT KID IN HIS RIGHT MIND WOULD WANT ONE OF THOSE!

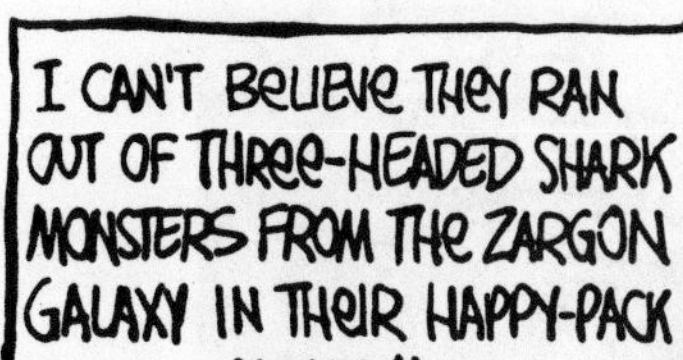

I CAN'T BELIEVE THEY RAN OUT OF THREE-HEADED SHARK MONSTERS FROM THE ZARGON GALAXY IN THEIR HAPPY-PACK MEALS!!

NICK LOVES THOSE ZARGON SHARK PEOPLE! ALL WEEK I TOLD HIM WE'D GET ONE FOR HIS COLLECTION!
BRIAN BASSET

LOOK, NICK. I KNOW YOU'RE HUNGRY...

BUT THEY WON'T DEFEAT US, BY GOLLY! WHY, WE'LL DRIVE ALL OVER TOWN IF WE HAVE TO UNTIL WE FIND A THREE-HEADED SHARK MONSTER!!

HOW WAS YOUR DAY, LAURA?
EXHAUSTING. I HAD TO MEET WITH A CLIENT OVER BREAKFAST THIS MORNING, AND ANOTHER CLIENT THIS AFTERNOON OVER LUNCH.

SOUNDS BRUTAL.

DO I NOTE A LITTLE SARCASM IN YOUR VOICE, ADAM?
BRIAN BASSET

ONLY A LITTLE? LET ME TRY THAT AGAIN...

ADAM
BY BRIAN BASSET
SCR EEEEEECH

SOUNDS LIKE LAURA'S BACK WITH THE KIDS.

HOW WAS YOUR TIME ALONE WITH THE KIDS?
AWFUL.

CLAYTON AND KATY BICKERED THE ENTIRE TIME...
NICK CRIED THROUGH THE MOVIE. BUT HEY— AT LEAST I COULD MAKE OUT SOME OF THE DIALOGUE EVERY TIME I STOOD OUT IN THE LOBBY WITH HIM.
DID NOT!
DID TOO!

THEN ON OUR WAY HOME WE STOPPED OFF FOR ICE CREAM. OF COURSE, IT ONLY GOT WORSE.

DID NOT!
DID TOO!
BRIAN BASSET

DAD, CAN I HAVE A RAISE IN MY ALLOWANCE?

YOU KNOW YOUR MOTHER CONTROLS THE FINANCES. ASK **HER**.

BUT YOU'RE SO WISE AND UNDERSTANDING.
BRIAN BASSET

SHE ALREADY SAID "NO," HUH?
SHE'S THINKING IT OVER.

TELL YOU WHAT, DAD— I'LL MAKE A DEAL WITH YOU.

IF YOU PUT A GOOD WORD IN FOR **ME** TO MOM WHILE SHE CONSIDERS RAISING MY ALLOWANCE...
YOU'LL KEEP YOUR ROOM TIDY?!!

HECK NO.
BRIAN BASSET

...I'LL GIVE YOU 1% OF MY NEW EARNINGS.

LET ME GET THIS STRAIGHT. **YOU** JUST ASKED YOUR MOM FOR A RAISE IN YOUR ALLOWANCE...

...**AND** YOU'LL GIVE ME **HOW MUCH AGAIN** IF I PUT IN A GOOD WORD FOR YOU?!
BRIAN BASSET

1% OF MY NEW EARNINGS!
WOW! THINK YOU CAN REALLY SPARE THAT MUCH?

SURE! I PROMISED KATY I'D GIVE HER **25%** FOR SAYING HOW NICE I'VE BEEN TO HER LATELY.

C'MON, DAD! I'M OFFERING YOU 1% OF WHATEVER KIND OF RAISE I GET IN MY ALLOWANCE FROM MOM IF YOU'LL JUST PUT IN A GOOD WORD FOR ME.
NO DEAL.

OH, I GET IT! 1% ISN'T ENOUGH FOR YOU! YOU WANT MORE, HUH?!!

BRIAN BASSET
EXTORTION! EXTORTION!

BRIAN BASSET

YOU JUST GAVE CLAYTON A RAISE IN HIS ALLOWANCE— SO WHY NOT MORE SPENDING MONEY FOR ME?!
CLAYTON GETS MOST OF HIS CHORES DONE.

BRIAN BASSET
SWITCH

HEY.
SWITCH

WE'RE NOT WATCHING THE SCRAMBLED STATIONS!
THEY WOULDN'T BE SCRAMBLED IF WE PAID FOR THEM!

BRIAN BASSET
WHAT'CHA WORKING ON, ADAM?
NOTHING.
DON'T TELL ME YOU'RE FILLING OUT ANOTHER ONE OF THOSE MAGAZINE SURVEYS ON LOVE AND MARRIAGE?
NO, JUST THE CROSSWORD PUZZLE.
QUESTION TWO: HOW HONEST ARE YOU WITH YOUR SPOUSE?
very.

QUESTION FOUR: HOW OFTEN DO YOU AND YOUR SPOUSE DINE BY CANDLE-LIGHT?

A) ONCE IN THE PAST YEAR.
B) TWICE IN THE PAST YEAR.
C) THREE OR MORE TIMES A YEAR.
BRIAN BASSET

LEMME SEE... THERE WAS THAT DISASTER OF A CAMPING TRIP LAST AUGUST... THAT BIG WINDSTORM IN MARCH... AND THEN TWO WEEKS AGO I BLEW THOSE FUSES...

C.

C'MON, GIVE ME A JUICY QUESTION TO ANSWER.
OKAY. HOW OFTEN DO YOU AND YOUR SPOUSE MAKE...
...TIME TO WATCH OLD RE-RUNS OF "MR. ED" TOGETHER?
WHAT KIND OF DUMB QUESTION RELATING TO LOVE AND MARRIAGE IS THAT??!
SO YOUR ANSWER IS?....
BRIAN BASSET
"NEVER".
THAT'S NOT GOOD. WE'RE DRIFTING APART.

BRIAN BASSET
QUESTION EIGHT: DOES YOUR SPOUSE TELL YOU EVERYTHING? DO YOU CONSIDER HIM OR HER COMPLETELY TRUSTWORTHY?
ABSOLUTELY!
SAME HERE!
OKAY, NEXT QUESTION.
HE'S LYING.
SHE'S LYING.
DO YOU AND YOUR SPOUSE EVER...

THIS MAGAZINE SURVEY SAYS OUR PASSION-METER IS LOW, THAT WE DON'T SPEND ENOUGH TIME TOGETHER, AND WE'RE NOT COMMUNICATING WELL.

JUST A SEC WHILE I TALLY UP OUR SCORE.

YOU DON'T THINK OUR MARRIAGE IS IN TROUBLE, DO YOU?

NOT ACCORDING TO THIS! IT HAS US SCORING IN THE UPPER TWO-THIRDS FOR TODAY'S COUPLES.

BRIAN BASSET

ADAM
BY BRIAN BASSET
ADAM, PUT THAT THING AWAY!

IN A MINUTE.
SWITCH

SHUT THE TV OFF AND GO TO SLEEP.
I JUST WANT TO WATCH THE NEWS.

DO IT DOWNSTAIRS, PLEASE. I HAVE AN IMPORTANT MEETING IN THE MORNING.
TELL YA WHAT— I'LL TURN THE VOLUME WAY DOWN.

NO, EVEN BETTER. I'LL HIT THE MUTE BUTTON AND READ LIPS.

AND I'LL SET THE BRIGHTNESS CONTROL ON THE PICTURE TO ITS LOWEST LEVEL— THEREBY EMITTING BARELY ANY LIGHT AT ALL!

FINE.
SCORE ONE FOR ME!...
...I THINK.

HOW 'BOUT PANCAKES THIS MORNING, DAD?
OK.

BRIAN BASSET
NO, FOR US! YOU'RE SUPPOSED TO MAKE THEM FOR US.
OH.

THE FOLLOWING PROGRAM CONTAINS SCENES AND LANGUAGE SOME VIEWERS MAY FIND OBJECTIONABLE.

BRIAN BASSET

ONE... TWO... THREE... GO!

HA! SCISSORS CAN'T CUT STONE. I WIN! YOU GET BATH DUTY TONIGHT!
WRONG. THESE SCISSORS ARE MADE OF A HIGH-TECH COMPOSITE ALLOY. THEY CAN CUT THROUGH ANYTHING.
BRIAN BASSET

BRIAN BASSET
WAHHHHH

WAHHHH

QUIET! TAKE YOUR NAP!

WAHHH

WHOA, HOLD VERY STILL, KATY.
BRIAN BASSET

GOT YOUR NOSE!
LOOK

DADDY. THAT'S THE OLDEST, DUMBEST TRICK IN THE WORLD.

RING

BRIAN BASSET
LAURA NEWMAN.

PANT-PANT-PANT-PANT-PANT-PANT...

ADAM, IS THAT YOU?
PANT-PANT-PANT-PANT-PANT PANT...

WELL, NICK! HERE WE ARE AT THE PARK!

AHHH, YES— NOTHING LIKE BEING AT THE PARK.

WHERE WE CAN... CAN...

BRIAN BASSET

PARK OURSELVES.

...6...5...4... 3...2...1...

WE HAVE LIFTOFF!
BRIAN BASSET

WE HAVE RE-ENTRY.

BRIAN BASSET

ARE YOU OK?
YEAH. WHAT HAPPENED?

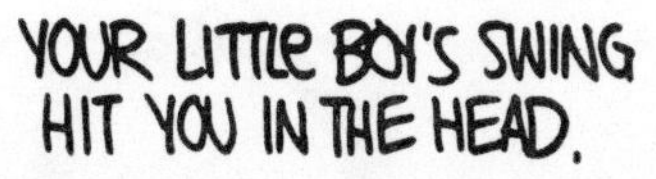
YOUR LITTLE BOY'S SWING HIT YOU IN THE HEAD.

BRIAN BASSET

YOU'RE SURE YOU'RE OK?
YEAH.

WHAT LITTLE BOY?

MY GOODNESS, WHAT HAPPENED TO YOU, ADAM?!
I GOT HIT IN THE HEAD AT THE PARK.
BRIAN BASSET

I'D HATE TO SEE THE OTHER GUY

THE OTHER GUY.

HOW ON EARTH DID YOU LET YOURSELF GET HIT IN THE HEAD BY A SWING, ADAM?

I WAS DISTRACTED. I TURNED TO LOOK AT THIS BEAUTIFUL WOM...
BRIAN BASSET

I CAN'T REMEMBER. IT'S ALL A BLANK!!

ADAM
BY BRIAN BASSET

BRIAN BASSET

I'M NOT EATING THIS GARBAGE! IT'S DISGUSTING!

PIZZA
AND WHEN YOU'RE READY TO EAT YOU CAN COME DOWN!

ADAM
BY BRIAN BASSET
SO WHAT DO YOU FEEL LIKE?
EITHER A ROTTEN PARENT FOR LEAVING THE KIDS TONIGHT...

...OR A HORRIBLY ROTTEN PARENT FOR LEAVING THE KIDS TONIGHT.

LAURA, WHAT'S WRONG?
I DUNNO. I SUPPOSE I FEEL BAD THAT WE LEFT THE KIDS TONIGHT.
DID YOU SEE THE LOOKS ON THEIR FACES WHEN WE WENT OUT THE DOOR?

LAURA, OUR KIDS LOVE TO LAY GUILT TRIPS. THEY'RE THE BEST IN THE BUSINESS! THEY WROTE THE BOOK ON IT.
TRUE. WE HAVEN'T BEEN OUT FOR A WHILE..

PARDON ME, MONSIEUR, MADAM, BUT YOUR BABY SITTER JUST PHONED AND NEEDS YOU HOME RIGHT AWAY.

THANK GOD YOU LEFT THE NUMBER OF THE RESTAURANT BY THE PHONE!
I HAD A FEELING SOMETHING BAD WOULD HAPPEN TONIGHT!!
BRIAN BASSET

THERE! THAT'LL TEACH 'EM NEVER TO ABANDON US FOR THE EVENING.
IT'S AWFULLY QUIET IN THERE. IS EVERYTHING OK?

DADDY, WHAT'S FOR DINNER?
CHINESE.

CHINESE? YOU'VE NEVER FIXED CHINESE FOOD BEFORE.
BRIAN BASSET

GUESS WHAT? DAD'S MAKING CHINESE FOOD FOR DINNER.

GREAT. JUST WHAT THE WORLD NEEDS— ANOTHER INTERNATIONAL INCIDENT.

HONEST! SOMEHOW I PICKED UP TWO ADULT VOICES THROUGH KELSEY'S NURSERY MONITOR! I SUPPOSE THAT MAYBE THIS (AHEM) RATHER ACTIVE AND INTIMATE COUPLE WERE CONVERSING LOUD ENOUGH THAT THEIR OWN CHILD'S MONITOR IN ANOTHER ROOM WAS ABLE TO BROADCAST IT.
YEAH, RIGHT. DID YOU CATCH ANY NAMES?

ONLY "SEXY SNOOKUMS" AND "HUNK-A-LUNK."
BRIAN BASSET

ADAM, WHAT'S SO URGENT THAT YOU LEFT SEVEN NOTES FOR ME TO CALL YOU?

LAURA. WE'RE BEING BUGGED!
SAY WHAT?

BUGGED!! APPARENTLY OUR MOST INTIMATE MOMENTS ARE BEING SOMEHOW PICKED UP AND BROADCAST THROUGH NICK'S NURSERY MONITOR FOR THE WHOLE NEIGHBORHOOD TO TUNE INTO!
BRIAN BASSET

C'MON, ADAM. HOW OFTEN CAN THAT BE?
OH, RIGHT.

ADAM, PUT THAT AWAY. BELIEVE ME. YOU'RE NOT GOING TO PICK UP OTHER PEOPLE'S CONVERSATIONS WITH THAT.

SHHHHH, I'M GETTING SOMETHING. I HEAR A DOG BARKING... A PLANE FLYING OVERHEAD...
SEE. I TOLD YOU YOU WOULDN'T GET ANYTHING JUICY.
BRIAN BASSET
ONLY IT'S **NOT** A DOG BARKING.

ADAM, THE BABY SITTER'S HERE!! COME ON, HUSTLE!

GEEESH. YOU'D THINK A MAN WHO STAYS HOME WITH KIDS ALL DAY WOULD BE EAGER TO GET OUT OF THE HOUSE.

BRIAN BASSET
ADAM!

ARE YOU COMING, LAURA?!! I'VE BEEN WAITING OUT IN THE CAR FOR 30 MINUTES!

WHAT RESTAURANT ARE WE MEETING KIM AND MARK AT?

WE'RE NOT. WE'RE HAVING DINNER AT THEIR PLACE.
BRIAN BASSET

WHAT?! I'M COOPED UP ALL DAY WITH KIDS, AND THEN WHEN I FINALLY DO GET OUT, YOU TELL ME IT'S TO GO TO ANOTHER COUPLE'S HOUSE WHO HAVE CHILDREN!

SOMETHING'S WRONG HERE.

YOU'RE RIGHT. I SHOULD'VE LEFT YOU WITH THE SITTER.

DELICIOUS STEW, KIM!
DON'T LOOK AT ME. MARK'S THE GOURMET IN THE FAMILY.

REALLY? UM...YES, VERY GOOD, MARK.

PSSST. IT WOULD BE NICE IF YOU'D COMPLIMENT MY EFFORTS IN THE KITCHEN ONCE IN A WHILE.

COULD ADAM HAVE YOUR RECIPE, MARK?
BRIAN BASSET

THAT WAS A WONDERFUL STEW MARK FIXED TONIGHT.
IT WAS OK.

OK?? ADAM NEWMAN, I BELIEVE YOU'RE JEALOUS OF MARK'S COOKING.
BRIAN BASSET
HARDLY! I'VE TASTED BETTER.
YEAH, WHEN?
LAST YEAR— WHEN THEY HAD US OVER BEFORE.

NO, REALLY. IF I DIDN'T KNOW YOU BETTER, ADAM, I'D SAY YOU WERE JEALOUS OF MARK'S COOKING SKILLS.

ME? JEALOUS? MAKE ME LAUGH.
WELL, YOU CERTAINLY WERE QUIET AT DINNER.

THAT'S BECAUSE I COULDN'T GET A WORD IN EDGEWISE.
BRIAN BASSET

...ALL YOU AND KIM DID WAS RAVE NON-STOP ABOUT WHAT A GREAT STEW MARK HAD FIXED... HOW TENDER THE VEGETABLES WERE... HOW CRISP THE SALAD WAS...

I CAN'T BELIEVE HOW COMPETITIVE YOU CAN GET SOMETIMES, ADAM. LIKE INVITING KIM AND MARK OVER FOR DINNER TOMORROW WHEN WE JUST HAD DINNER AT THEIR PLACE.
WHAT'S COMPETITIVE ABOUT THAT?? I'M JUST RECIP-ROCATING THEIR OFFER.
BRIAN BASSET
ADAM. I KNOW YOU. YOU JUST WANT TO PROVE ONE THING... THAT YOU'RE JUST AS GOOD A COOK AS MARK.
THERE YOU'RE WRONG.

I WANT TO MAKE HIM BEG FOR SECONDS.

WHAT CULINARY MASTERPIECE HAVE YOU CHOSEN TO IMPRESS OUR FRIENDS WITH TONIGHT?
I'M GOING TO BARBECUE A SALMON.

COULD BE RISKY, ADAM. NOT EVERYONE LIKES FISH, Y'KNOW.

I THOUGHT OF THAT.
BRIAN BASSET

SO I BOUGHT A SMALL SALMON.

THIS IS SURE NICE OF YOU AND ADAM TO HAVE US OVER SO SOON.
YES.
WELL, WE HAD SUCH AN ENJOYABLE EVEN-ING AT YOUR PLACE.

WHERE IS THE CULINARY ARTIST?

ON THE DECK BARBECUING A SALMON.
MMM- SOUNDS EXQUISITE!
BRIAN BASSET

BE RIGHT BACK! JUST GOTTA RUN TO THE STORE FOR SOME TARTAR SAUCE!

BE RIGHT BACK! JUST GOTTA RUN TO THE STORE FOR SOME TARTAR SAUCE!

AND DON'T WORRY ABOUT DINNER. I'VE GOT EVERYTHING COVERED.
BRIAN BASSET

SORRY I'M LATE. CAN YOU BELIEVE IT— I HAD TO GO TO THREE STORES TO FIND TARTAR SAUCE.
BRIAN BASSET

HEY. WHERE ARE MARK AND KIM?
THE SALMON?!

ARRGGHH—AND THE SALMON'S BURNT TO A CRISP!
PHOOOOOF!

MARK AND KIM HAD TO GO HOME. THEIR BABY SITTER PHONED AND JESSE'S RUNNING A HIGH FEVER.
THANK YOU THANK YOU THANK YOU.

YES SIREE—JUST LOOK AT THAT FLOOR SHINE!

HERE COMES LAURA NOW. LET'S SEE IF SHE NOTICES.

AAAAAAA

BRIAN BASSET
SMASH

ADAM
BY BRIAN BASSET

BRIAN BASSET

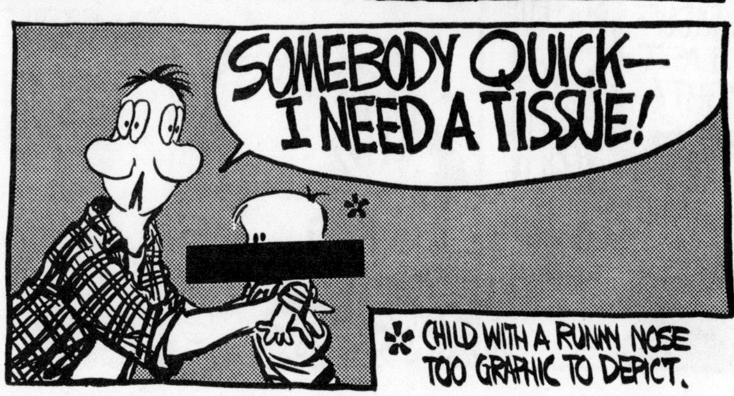
SOMEBODY QUICK—
I NEED A TISSUE!
*
* CHILD WITH A RUNNY NOSE
TOO GRAPHIC TO DEPICT.

ADDY, MY OOTH IS OOSE.
WELL, DON'T PULL IT OUT.

UT IT'S IGGLING ACK AND ORTH.
DON'T PULL IT OUT.

UT IT ONTS TO UM OUT.
DON'T PULL IT.
BRIAN BASSET

THERE! IT'S OUT!
ARRGG, GROSS! DON'T SHOW IT TO ME!

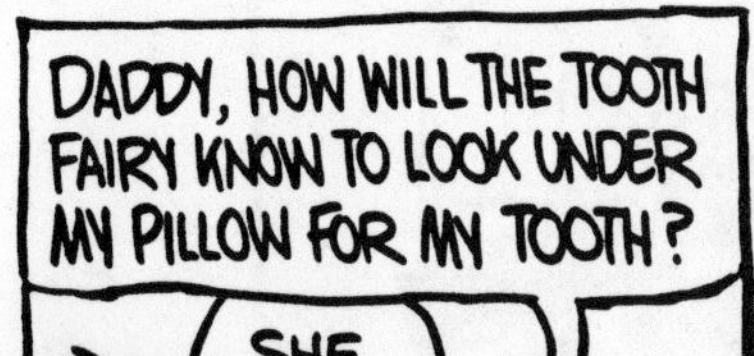
DADDY, HOW WILL THE TOOTH FAIRY KNOW TO LOOK UNDER MY PILLOW FOR MY TOOTH?
SHE JUST DOES, HONEY.

OK, BUT WHAT IF SHE FORGETS TO COME?!

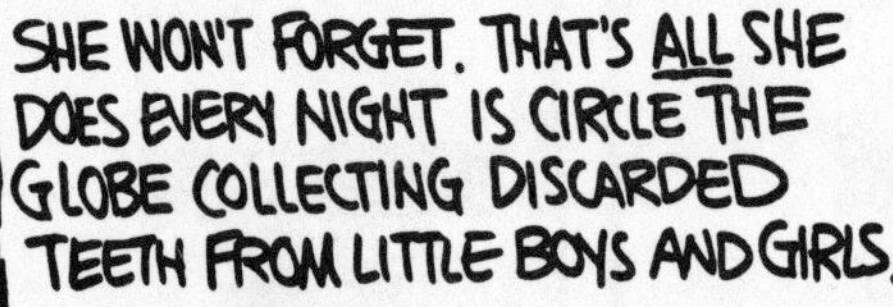
SHE WON'T FORGET. THAT'S ALL SHE DOES EVERY NIGHT IS CIRCLE THE GLOBE COLLECTING DISCARDED TEETH FROM LITTLE BOYS AND GIRLS.

BRIAN BASSET

WHAT AN AWFUL JOB.

WAHHHHH, THE TOOTH FAIRY DIDN'T COME LAST NIGHT!
BRIAN BASSET

SMACK!

NO, SHE CAME TO THE HOUSE LAST NIGHT, KATY. SHE DIDN'T FORGET YOU. IT'S JUST THAT... THAT...
SNIFF
...DADDY FORGOT TO DE-PROGRAM THE BURGLAR ALARM SYSTEM, AND SHE MISTAKENLY GOT HAULED AWAY BY THE POLICE FOR TRYING TO GET IN.
OH.

ADAM, WAKE UP!

THE KIDS HAVEN'T EATEN YET... NICK NEEDS A NEW DIAPER... KATY HAS A DENTAL APPOINT-MENT THIS MORNING, AND I HAVE TO RUN OR I'LL BE LATE TO THE OFFICE.

OK, I'M UP–I'M UP! NOW HAVE A GOOD DAY OF VACATION.

VACATION?? YOU MEAN "WORK."
IT'S ALL HOW YOU INTERPRET IT.
BRIAN BASSET

BRIAN BASSET

I'M TELLING YOU, LAURA. THE KIDS... THEY RUN ME INTO THE GROUND.
BRIAN BASSET

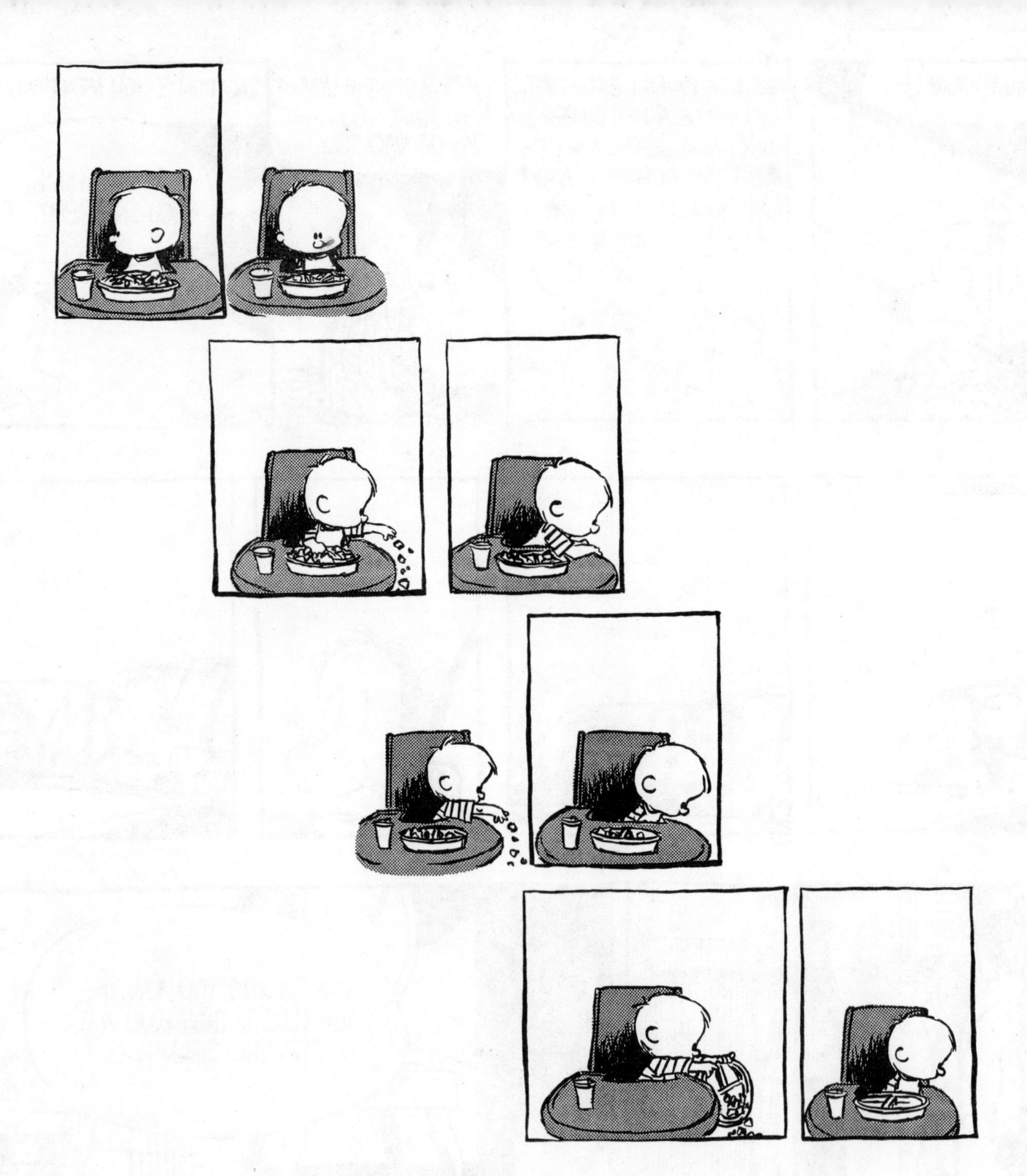

THE END